South Bay Bike Trails

Road and Mountain Bicycle Rides throughout Santa Clara and Santa Cruz Counties

D1015292

by
Conrad J. Boisvert

Penngrove Publications
P.O. Box 1017
Penngrove, CA 94951
www.penngrovepub.com

For Bonnie

Library of Congress Catalog Card Number 90-62590
International Standard Book Number 0-9621694-8-X

Cover photograph by Bob Morris
Taken on West Cliff Drive in Santa Cruz
Cyclists: Conrad Boisvert and Bonnie Reyling

Printed in the United States of America

First printing, September 1990
Second printing, October 1993
Second Edition, March 2000
Fourth printing, May 2001

Penngrove Publications
P.O. Box 1017
Penngrove, CA 94951
www.penngrovepub.com

TABLE OF CONTENTS

Explore the South Bay by Bike! 5
Regions of the South Bay 6
San Francisco South Bay Area 7
How to Use This Book 8

Rides
Santa Clara Valley: East Foothills 10
   1. San Felipe Valley and Metcalf Road 11
   2. New Almaden and Hicks Road Loop 14
   3. Coyote Creek Bike Path 18
   4. Quimby Road Loop 21
   5. Sierra Road Loop 24
   6. Grant Ranch County Park 27

Santa Clara Valley: West Foothills 31
   7. Saratoga and Stevens Canyon Back Roads 32
   8. Tour of Los Gatos and Saratoga Foothills 35
   9. Los Gatos Creek Trail 39
  10. Los Gatos and Castle Rock Loop 43
  11. Sierra Azul Open Space Preserve 46
  12. St. Joseph's Hill Open Space Preserve 49

Santa Cruz Area: Mountains and Beaches 53
  13. Los Gatos and Soquel Loop 54
  14. Santa Cruz and Capitola Beach Ride 57
  15. Eureka Canyon and Soquel Loop 60
  16. Seacliff Beach and Corralitos Loop 63
  17. Soquel Demonstration Forest 66
  18. The Forest of Nisene Marks and Sand Point Overlook 69

West Santa Cruz Area: Mountains and Forests 73
  19. Empire Grade and Bonny Doon 74
  20. Zayante Road and Bear Creek Road Loop 77
  21. Felton Empire Road 80
  22. Big Basin and Castle Rock Loop 83
  23. Big Basin Redwoods State Park 86
  24. Wilder Ranch State Historic Preserve 90

South County: Ranches and Farms 94
  25. Chesbro and Uvas Reservoirs 95
  26. Gilroy Hot Springs and Cañada Road 98
  27. Corralitos and Green Valley Loop 102
  28. Rio Del Mar — Watsonville Loop 106
  29. Pajaro Valley and the Elkhorn Slough 109
  30. Henry Coe State Park Out-and-Back 112
  31. Henry Coe State Park — Kelly Lake 115

Appendix
Rides by Ratings 120
Mountain Bike Rides 121
Points of Interest 122
Bicycling Tips 124
About the Author 127
The Bay Area Bike Trails Series 128

ACKNOWLEDGMENTS

My sincere thanks goes out to all the cycling partners I have had over the years who have had the patience to withstand the many exploratory routes I have been inclined to try. Among them, in no particular order, are Sue Johnson, Dennis Vanata, Kathy Picard, Robert Warman, Richard Wong, Laurie Nierenberg, Jean Newton, Bob Godwin, Klaus Schumann, Kellie Reed, Tim Bussey, Oleg Vizir, Gregg and Linda Fussell, Jim Smothers, and Clari Nolet. I especially appreciate their patience with me, as together we conquered many hills that we sometimes expected and other times were surprised and maybe a little dismayed by them.

Bonnie Reyling deserves special mention for putting up with my idiosyncrasies and for making my life more wonderful than I thought possible. Thanks also to my terrific children, Judie, Charles, and Steve, for their ongoing moral support and encouragement.

Bob Morris deserves recognition for his wonderful cover photograph which captures the joy and exhilaration of the sport of recreational cycling so well. Finally, this book would have been much more difficult to complete without the ongoing support, encouragement, and prodding of my publisher, Phyllis Neumann. Without her, I can only wonder whether I would have written the book or not. For this, I am exceedingly grateful.

Along Summit Road

EXPLORE THE SOUTH BAY BY BIKE!

As both the birthplace of the mountain bike and the training ground for numerous world-class bicycle racers, the San Francisco Bay Area has long been one of the premier places for recreational cycling. The dramatic mountain ranges framing the Bay Area, caused by the pressures at the juncture of the earth's tectonic plates, provide both a scenic backdrop and a vertical challenge for those two-wheel fanatics eager enough to go at them.

The South Bay, best known for its image as "Silicon Valley", the home of high-tech and high pressure jobs, is also a paradise for cyclists of all abilities. Away from the busy city streets and freeways, the surrounding countryside offers a wide variety of scenery and historical places to stimulate both the body and mind.

The eastern boundary of the South Bay, at least as far as this book is concerned, is the range of foothills beneath 4,000 foot high Mount Hamilton. To the south, the area extends into the farms and ranches of Morgan Hill and continues farther south to Gilroy. Along the Pacific coast edge of the South Bay, the southernmost edge is the Elkhorn Slough, near Watsonville and the northernmost is Bonny Doon, a small community slightly north of Santa Cruz. Back across the mountains into the heart of the Santa Clara Valley, the northern edge of the South Bay is around Cupertino.

The variety of terrain and micro-climates is what sets the Bay Area apart from nearly all other places on earth. On any given day it is possible to ride the roads or trails through golden hills dotted with oak trees and on the next, to ride through thick redwood forests shrouded in cool fog drifting in off the Pacific. Riding along the cliffs and beaches in Santa Cruz can be followed up by riding remote country roads through ranch land in and around Gilroy. Roads around Corralitos lead through apple orchards while those along the coast pass alongside artichoke or strawberry fields.

Migrating birds of many varieties can be seen in the Elkhorn Slough at certain times of the year. At other times, the monarch butterflies find their way to their sanctuary at Natural Bridges State Park in Santa Cruz. Wild pigs, turkeys, and golden eagles can frequently be sighted in the hills east of Gilroy.

The rides in *South Bay Bike Trails* have been carefully chosen to appeal to cyclists of all abilities. There are assorted "easy" rides for the beginner, intermediate rides for those with a little more energy, and difficult rides for those looking for the challenge and rewards of bigger hills and longer distances. In all cases, the routes have been selected to provide the best scenery and the most safety. Get out there and enjoy the beauty of this wonderful area in which we are blessed to live!

REGIONS OF THE SOUTH BAY

Santa Clara Valley: East Foothills

East of the city of San Jose lies majestic Mount Hamilton and its famous Lick Observatory. In the foothills below, the roads lead through rural areas occupied by ranches and pasture land and offer pastoral scenes which can be a soothing antidote to the high pressures of the Silicon Valley workplace. The summertime can be quite hot in this part of the South Bay, but the spring and fall are delightful and are usually the best times for cycling.

Santa Clara Valley: West Foothills

In sharp contrast to the east foothills, the western part of the valley is heavily wooded, the rich redwood forests thriving by virtue of the cool, damp air coming in off the Pacific Ocean. Summers can be considerably cooler than the east foothills, due both to the abundant shade and the cooler air. Winter days can be brisk and ice can often form at the higher elevations. The towns of Saratoga and Los Gatos are focal points for cyclists and Sunday mornings usually find throngs of riders in the coffee shops before their rides.

Santa Cruz Area: Mountains and Beaches

The beach environment of this region contrasts sharply with the urban and suburban flavor of the population centers just over the hill. The resort town of Santa Cruz with its nearby U.C. campus, gives it a youthful and vigorous energy level, especially in the summer months. Despite the sometimes crowded and hectic nature of the place, numerous bike lanes offer the cyclist a substantial level of safety.

West Santa Cruz Area: Mountains and Forests

West of Santa Cruz is a hidden jewel for cyclists, for the roads here tend to carry little car traffic and follow through some of the most beautiful forests to be found in the entire Bay Area. The hills are substantial and there are few flat routes, but the scenery and remoteness are the ultimate rewards.

South County: Ranches and Farms

The South County has a wide variety of routes, even within itself. On the coast, roads lead through the farms and orchards around Watsonville and Corralitos, along the shores of the Elkhorn Slough, and into foothills filled with redwoods and ferns. Inland, on the other side of the mountains, lies the rural ranches of Gilroy and Morgan Hill, where the pleasant aromas often include garlic and onions, for which the area is known.

SAN FRANCISCO SOUTH BAY AREA

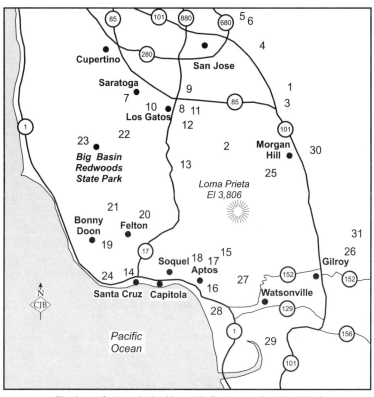

(Numbers refer to particular rides and indicate approximate locations)

HOW TO USE THIS BOOK

Understanding the Ride Parameters

At the beginning of each ride description is a short list of ride parameters. These are intended to give you a brief summary of that particular ride and to permit you to quickly select the ride that most suits what you are looking for.

Ride Rating — Reflects the overall difficulty of the ride, a simple judgment that classifies it into one of three categories: Easy, Moderate, or Difficult. The rating results from an evaluation of both the distance and elevation gain for the ride and is also influenced by the steepness of the hills.

Total Distance — Indicates the length of the ride, excluding any optional side trips that might be included in the ride description.

Riding Time — Gives an indication of how much time to allow for the ride. Keep in mind however, that this does not include extended stops for sightseeing, eating, or rests. The riding time usually assumes a moderate pace of about 8-10 miles an hour for most types of terrain and a slower pace for harder rides.

Total Elevation Gain — Combines the total elevation gain for all the hills along the route.

Calories Burned — Approximates the total amount of energy burned. This is based upon an average burn rate of about 300 calories per hour on a flat road at 14 miles an hour and about 800 calories an hour on a hill climb with an 8% grade and a speed of 4 miles an hour. Some variations occur for individual differences and for external factors, but this can be a rough guide to the overall difficulty of the ride.

Type of Bike — Suggests either road or mountain bike, depending on the route. Although a ride may have a stretch along a dirt section, it still may be suitable for a road bike, if it is smooth and safe.

Terrain

The roads conditions and general nature of the hills along the route are described in this paragraph in order to permit a quick peak as to the effort to be expected. Often a ride will be best at certain times of the year, in which case this will be detailed.

Ride Description

This section outlines a general description of the ride along with any interesting background or historical information about the area. The route to be followed is explained, although the details are covered more fully in the *Ride Details and Mile Markers* section. Extra side trip or ride variations are sometimes outlined in order to enhance the ride.

Starting Point

The exact place to start the ride is described, along with detailed directions explaining how to get there. In general, rides are started at locations where free parking is readily available and where refreshments can be obtained. Typically the starting points are also easily recognizable places, simplifying the situation for a group of people meeting to ride together. On maps, the starting points are indicated with **✱**.

Elevation Profile

The elevation profile provides a detailed view of the hills along the route. These not only preview the ride for you, but can be useful on the ride to help you anticipate the terrain ahead of you.

Map

Each ride has a map associated with it indicating the route. Rides with more than one route are indicated with direction arrows for each route.

Ride Details and Mile Markers

Directions for the route are described along with elapsed distances. You don't need a cycle computer for following the route, since the markers come at frequent intervals and you will quickly learn to estimate distances accurately enough. The required turns to take are clearly indicated. Special sights or points of interest along the way are also indicated.

Easy Ride Options

Some rides have optional easy routes. To keep them simple, they are usually set up as turn around points along a longer route. They are indicated in the ride summary at the beginning of each ride and in the *Ride Details and Mile Markers* section.

Wilder Ranch in Santa Cruz

Santa Clara Valley: East Foothills

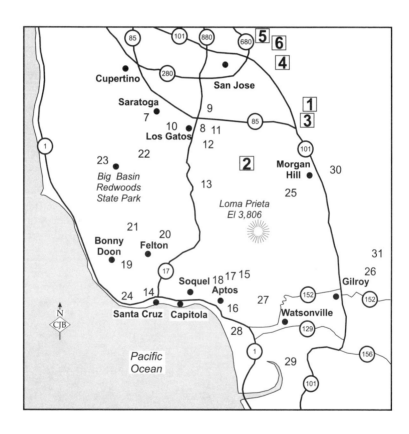

1 SAN JOSE
San Felipe Valley and Metcalf Road

Region: *Santa Clara Valley East*
Total Distance: *22 miles*
Total Elevation Gain: *1600 feet*
Type of Bike: *Road Bike*

Ride Rating: *Moderate*
Riding Time: *2-3 hours*
Calories Burned: *800*
Easy Option: *12 flat miles*

Terrain

The beginning of the ride is along a quiet paved bike path sometimes littered a bit with branches and leaves. The roads are generally lightly traveled and well-paved, although they also lack a wide shoulder. This ride is good any time of year, however hot summer days may be somewhat uncomfortable. Sections of the bike path can be flooded after heavy winter rains.

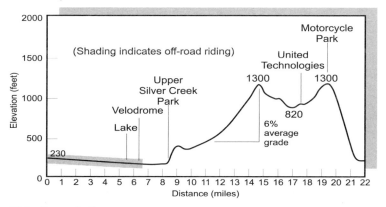

Ride Description

San Felipe Valley is just east of downtown San Jose, at the base of Mount Hamilton. The farms and ranches along the route offer many pastoral scenes for the bicyclist, even though recent residential development seems to be ongoing. The apparent remoteness and peacefulness of the area stand in stark contrast to the bustling city, so near and yet seemingly so far away.

The ride starts at a public parking area along the Coyote Creek Trail, a paved multi-use bike path. After passing through Hellyer Park, surface roads are used to take you into the Silver Creek Valley and through the recently developed residential community there. A steady climb along San Felipe Road leads you through eucalyptus trees into the country. Frequent shade and a gentle grade combine to make this one of the better hill climbs for novice and low-intermediate cyclists.

After the first summit, a short downhill takes you to the intersection with Metcalf Road. A shorter climb along Metcalf Road brings you past the Santa Clara County Motorcycle Park, a place for off-road motorcycles to make lots of noise and raise clouds of dust. The final downhill back to the starting point is quite steep and extra caution should be taken on the sharp hairpin turns along the way.

Starting Point

Start the ride at a parking area on Monterey Highway, near Metcalf Road. To get there, take Highway 85 south or Highway 101 south. At the point where these two highways meet, look for exit signs for Monterey Road. Get on Monterey Road and follow it south toward Morgan Hill. At Metcalf Road, make a u-turn and look for the parking area on the right side.

Ride Details and Mile Markers

0.0 Proceed NORTH along the Coyote Creek Trail.

1.6 Cross under Silicon Valley Boulevard.

3.3 Turn right on the old, unmarked road, cross the bridge and turn left to get back on the bike path.

5.2 Highway 101 underpass.

5.4 Hellyer Park Lake on the right side.

6.1 Velodrome on the left side. This is the site of Friday night bike races on the oval track. **EASY OPTION:** Return from this point.

Bridge on San Felipe Road

6.4 Just after passing the velodrome, proceed up the gravel section and out the gate onto Sylvandale Avenue. Make the first RIGHT turn onto Brock Way and then RIGHT again onto Yerba Buena Road.

7.3 Highway 101 underpass.

7.9 Old Silver Creek Road on the right side. This is the Upper Silver Creek Park and there are public restrooms available here.

8.6 Another stretch of Old Silver Creek Road on the right side.

9.0 Turn RIGHT onto Silver Creek Valley Road.

10.3 Turn LEFT onto Farnsworth Road.

11.0 Turn RIGHT onto San Felipe Road.

14.9 Crest of the hill.

15.9 Turn RIGHT onto Metcalf Road.

17.5 United Technologies facility on the left side.

19.5 Crest if the hill. County Motorcycle Park on the left side. Begin very steep descent.

22.2 Back at the start point.

Extra Option on San Felipe Road (2 miles out-and-back)

At the 15.9 mile point is the intersection with Metcalf Road. At this point there is a very pleasant side trip to the end of San Felipe Road, about 2 miles distant. Bear left to stay on San Felipe Road and continue a short distance to the intersection with Los Animas Road, where you will bear left again. Near this intersection is the abandoned Highland School, a small one-room structure. At the end of the road is the San Felipe Ranch, at which point you must turn around and return to the regular route.

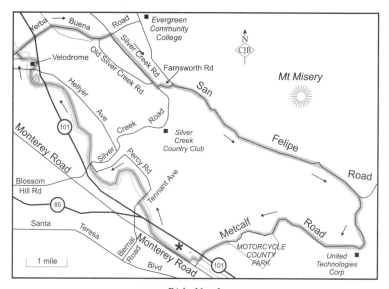

Ride No. 1

2 SAN JOSE
New Almaden and Hicks Road Loop

Region: *Santa Clara Valley East*
Total Distance: *19 miles*
Total Elevation Gain: *1300 feet*
Type of Bike: *Road Bike*

Ride Rating: *Moderate*
Riding Time: *2-3 hours*
Calories Burned: *700*

Terrain

The majority of this ride is along country roads with one significant hill to climb. The ride is good any time of year, although it is best in the spring, when the creeks are running and the hills are green.

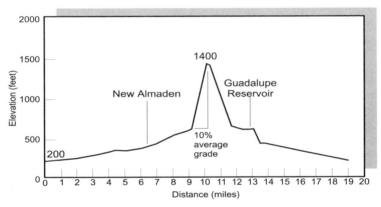

Ride Description

New Almaden was originally named after the city of Almaden in south-central Spain (about 100 miles south of Madrid) and has long been known for its rich, dark red earth which the native Indians of the area called "moketka." In 1824, Don Antonio Suñol began working a mining operation, thinking that the soil contained large quantities of silver. He abandoned these efforts when he concluded that no silver was present. Mining ceased completely until 1845, when Andres Castillero discovered that the red earth contained quicksilver, another name for mercury.

Although mining no longer takes place, New Almaden has retained its pioneer flavor and is a throwback to previous times, despite its close proximity to San Jose's suburban sprawl and high-tech image.

This ride takes you from the Almaden Plaza Shopping Center to New Almaden along busy Almaden Expressway. After passing through New Almaden, you will go up a small hill to the Almaden Dam and

Reservoir. Continuing past the reservoir, you will climb a rather steep grade along Hicks Road to the crest of the big hill. The descent will afford you some panoramic views of the valley ahead of you as it winds its way down to the Guadalupe Dam and Reservoir and continues along the Guadalupe Creek back to your start point.

Starting Point

The ride starts at the Almaden Plaza Shopping Center at the intersection of Blossom Hill Road and Almaden Expressway. To get there from areas north of San Jose, take Highway 85 south and get off at the exit for Almaden Expressway. From points south of San Jose, take Highway 85 north toward Mountain View and get off at Almaden Expressway. Go south on Almaden Expressway to the Blossom Hill Road intersection and park where it is convenient.

Ride Details and Mile Markers

0.0 Proceed SOUTH on Almaden Expressway.

0.8 Cross Coleman Road.

1.8 Cross Redmond Avenue.

2.5 Cross Camden Avenue.

4.3 Turn RIGHT onto Almaden Road. Almaden Expressway continues to the left.

4.9 Mockingbird Hill Lane is on the right. If you proceed down this road, you will come to one of the access points into Almaden Quicksilver Park. Bikes are not permitted on the trails in the park, but you may wish to explore on foot.

6.8 Opry House is on the left. This is a New Almaden landmark. Melodramas and a rustic western-style bar are featured here.

7.0 Town of New Almaden. There is a small mining museum on the left side part way through town.

7.2 Another entrance to Almaden Quicksilver Park on the right side. A California State Historic Landmark sign is on the left. The road becomes Alamitos Road at this point.

7.6 Almaden Dam and Reservoir on the left.

8.9 Turn RIGHT onto Hicks Road.

10.6 Crest of the hill at the intersection with Loma Almaden Road on the left side.

13.3 Guadalupe Dam and Reservoir on the right side.

15.5 Bear RIGHT at the intersection with Shannon Road.

17.0 Turn RIGHT onto Camden Avenue and then make an immediate LEFT onto Coleman Road.

18.6 Turn LEFT onto Almaden Expressway.

19.0 Back at the start point.

Extra Option on Loma Almaden Road (2 miles out-and-back)

At the crest of Hicks Road is the intersection with Loma Almaden Road. If you take this out-and-back side trip, you will climb about 900 feet over the 2-mile length of the road, with a portion of it very steep (about 17% for a section of 0.2 miles). You will reach a gate where you can park your bike and walk along a trail off to the left for some spectacular views of the canyons below Mt. Umunum, ahead and off to the right. This area is part of the Sierra Azul Open Space Preserve.

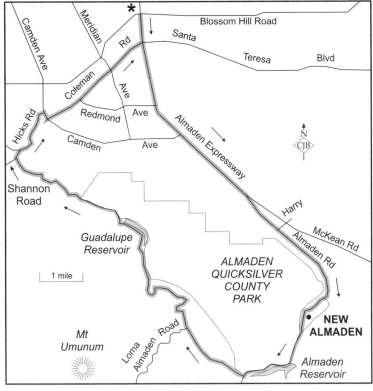

Ride No. 2

Opry House in New Almaden ⇨

3 SAN JOSE
Coyote Creek Bike Path

Region: *Santa Clara Valley East*
Total Distance: *31 miles*
Total Elevation Gain: *400 feet*
Type of Bike: *Road Bike*

Ride Rating: *Easy*
Riding Time: *2-3 hours*
Calories Burned: *700*
Easy Option: *13 flat miles*

Terrain

The bike path is paved, but slightly uneven in places. Debris, like small branches, leaves, and gravel, may be present and flooding sometimes occurs along sections of the trail after a heavy rainfall. A road bike is adequate, but a mountain bike might give some more protection against tire punctures. The ride is fairly flat and easily qualifies as one of the easiest in the South Bay.

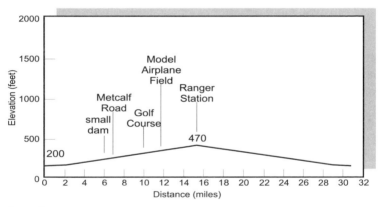

Ride Description

Hellyer Park, in San Jose, is the site of the Hellyer Park velodrome, one of three bicycle race tracks in California. Originally built for the Pan American Games of 1962, it was not actually completed until 1963. More recently, it has been the site of the 1972 Olympic Bike Trials and numerous California State Championship races. In the summer months, the velodrome hosts Friday night races which feature local cyclists of world-class caliber.

The start of the Coyote Creek Bike Path is near the velodrome in Hellyer Park. While there are other access points, this spot is one of the end points for the route and is a good place to begin. The bike path follows along the Coyote Creek to its source at the base of the Anderson Dam, just outside of Morgan Hill. The return is back along the same route. The distance to the other end is about 15.5 miles, but those looking for a shorter ride can easily turn around at any point.

The bike path can be accessed from near the velodrome. From the velodrome, proceed out toward the park exit and look for a dirt path on the right side. This will lead you onto the bike path. From there, simply follow it all the way to its end at a ranger station 15.5 miles distant. Be sure to stop along the way to experience the many unique sights on the splendid trail.

Starting Point

To get to Hellyer Park, go south on Highway 101 from San Jose. Get off at the Hellyer Avenue exit and go directly into Hellyer Coyote County Park. Continue straight ahead past the gate to the end of the road, where the velodrome is located.

Ride Details and Mile Markers

0.0 Leave the velodrome parking area the way you came in.

0.2 Turn onto the bike path just past the restroom on the side.

0.7 Lake on the left side.

1.0 Highway 101 underpass.

3.2 Cross under Silver Creek Valley Road and then cross a bridge over the creek to get back on the bike path on the far side.

4.9 Cross under Silicon Valley Boulevard.

5.6 Another Highway 101 underpass.

6.6 Boat launch on left side. **EASY OPTION:** Return from this point.

6.7 Cross over bridge and then cross over Metcalf Road to continue on bike path.

7.7 Turn LEFT onto a road for a short distance and then turn RIGHT to get back on the bike path.

10.0 Golf course on the left side.

11.3 Cross the creek over the bridge.

12.8 Turn LEFT at the road to follow the bike path.

13.3 Santa Clara County Model Aircraft Skypark on the left side. This is an interesting place to observe model airplane enthusiasts fly their planes.

14.1 Highway 101 underpass.

14.8 The Oak Rest Area. Although the trail continues, this is the turn-around point for this ride. Retrace your route back to Hellyer Park.

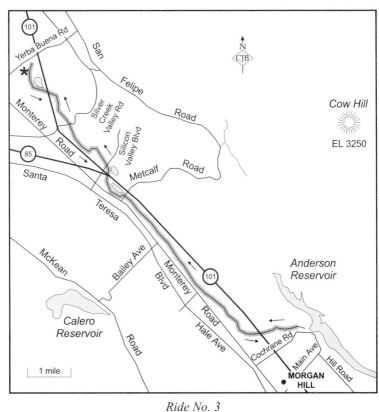

Ride No. 3

Scene along Coyote Creek Bike Path

4   SAN JOSE
Quimby Road Loop

Region: *Santa Clara Valley East*
Total Distance: *21 miles*
Total Elevation Gain: *2200 feet*
Type of Bike: *Road Bike*

Ride Rating: *Difficult*
Riding Time: *2-3 hours*
Calories Burned: *900*

Terrain

The majority of the route is along country roads with one sustained hill climb. The ride is good any time of year, although it is best in the spring and fall when it is less likely to be hot.

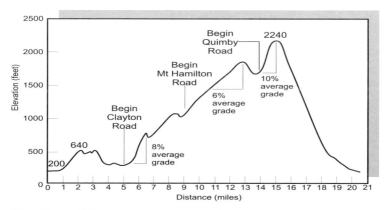

Ride Description

Mount Hamilton is the highest peak in the Bay Area and represents one of the toughest challenges for cyclists. This route does not go all the way up the mountain, but instead follows Clayton Road to Mt. Hamilton Road and then follows Mt. Hamilton Road to Grant Ranch County Park, part way up the mountain. From there another climb along Quimby Road to an elevation of 2,240 feet is followed by a steep descent back to the start point.

The ride starts near the community of Evergreen in the east side of San Jose. The corner of Quimby Road and White Road has ample parking opportunities nearby.

The route initially leads east along Quimby Road. Traveling north on Mt. Pleasant Road, the route runs along the base of the foothills as it winds its way toward Clayton Road. Clayton Road is a winding road which climbs through less populated countryside and intersects Mt. Hamilton Road. Mt. Hamilton Road climbs less steeply until it crests and descends a small amount into Hall's Valley and leads to Grant Ranch County Park. Quimby Road has another relatively steep climb before the final crest at the gates for Buckeye Ranch. The descent is fast and steep as the road leads back into the Santa Clara Valley. The roads are all well paved but lack wide shoulders.

Starting Point

A good place to begin this ride is at the intersection of White Road and Quimby Road where several shopping centers are. To get there, proceed south from San Jose on Highway 101. Take the Capitol Expressway exit and head east on Capitol Expressway to get to Quimby Road. Turn right on Quimby Road and follow it until you get to White Road.

Ride Details and Mile Markers

0.0   Proceed EAST along Quimby Road.

1.6   Turn LEFT onto Murillo Avenue.

2.2   Turn RIGHT onto Mt. Pleasant Road.

4.5   Continue STRAIGHT across Marten Avenue.

5.0   Turn RIGHT onto Clayton Road and begin climbing up the winding road.

6.0   Orchards on the right side.

9.4   Turn RIGHT sharply onto Mt. Hamilton Road. Grade becomes relatively gentle.

12.8   Crest of the hill — 1,900 feet.

14.4   Turn RIGHT onto Quimby Road. Prepare for steep grade.

15.5   Crest of the hill at Buckeye Ranch — 2,240 feet.

15.6   Begin steep descent.

18.7   Begin residential area.

19.8   Continue STRAIGHT at intersection with Ruby Road.

20.6   Back at the start point.

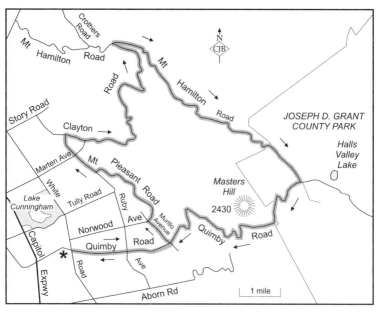

Ride No. 4

Along Mount Hamilton Road

5 SAN JOSE
Sierra Road Loop

Region: *Santa Clara Valley East*
Total Distance: *16 miles*
Total Elevation Gain: *2200 feet*
Type of Bike: *Road Bike*

Ride Rating: *Difficult*
Riding Time: *2-3 hours*
Calories Burned: *900*
Easy Option: *6 flat miles*

Terrain

This ride follows mostly quiet country roads in the hills around Milpitas. There is some car traffic along Piedmont Road and Calaveras Road early in the ride. A substantial hill climb gets you up to about 2,000 feet for some spectacular views.

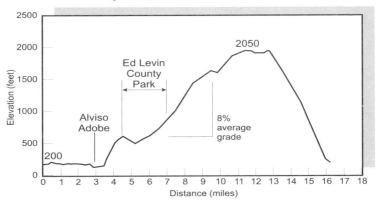

Ride Description

The Calaveras Valley, while so near to the big population centers of the Bay Area, can at the same time seem so far away. Nestled beyond the foothills in the eastern part of the South Bay, the valley forms a basin which collects water for the Calaveras Reservoir.

The route of this ride will take you along the base of the foothills on Piedmont Road through residential areas of Milpitas. It will then follow Old Calaveras Road and then Calaveras Road as it climbs through Ed Levin County Park, an area noted for its fine hiking and equestrian trails. Continuing to climb past the park, panoramic vistas reveal the beauty of the Calaveras Valley and Reservoir far below and in the distance. Continuing through ranch land and rural residential areas, the roads come back around toward the populated Santa Clara Valley with ever changing views all along the way. The final descent back into the valley brings you back to the point at which you began.

Starting Point

Start the ride at the intersection of Piedmont Road and Sierra Road in San Jose. To get there, take the Berryessa Road exit off Highway 680 and follow Berryessa Road east. Turn left onto Capitol Avenue and go for about ½-mile to Sierra Road. Turn right onto Sierra Road and follow it to the intersection with Piedmont Road and begin the ride there.

Ride Details and Mile Markers

0.0   Proceed NORTH along Piedmont Road.

3.1   Continue STRAIGHT onto Evans Road at the intersection with Calaveras Road. Historic Alviso Adobe is about 0.1 miles to the right along Calaveras Road. **EASY OPTION:** Return from this point.

3.5   Turn RIGHT onto Old Calaveras Road and begin steep climb for a short distance.

4.6   Sign indicating Ed Levin County Park at the crest of the hill.

4.8   Turn RIGHT onto Downing Road. Golf course will then be on the left side.

5.1   Turn LEFT onto Calaveras Road.

5.7   Restrooms on the right side.

6.3   Continue STRAIGHT at the intersection with Weller Road on the left.

6.5   Continue STRAIGHT to begin Felter Road as Calaveras Road turns to the left.

7.4   Continue STRAIGHT at intersection with Marsh Road on the left.

9.5   Brief respite from the climb. Enjoy the short descent and then resume climbing.

11.6   Crest of the hill. This is the highest point along the route — 2,050 feet.

12.6   Begin descent — very steep in places, so watch your speed.

16.3   Back at the start point.

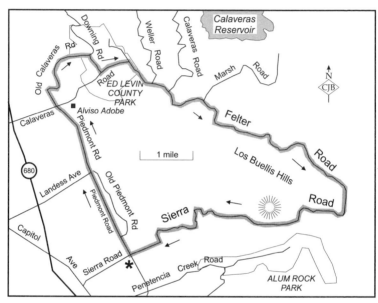

Ride No. 5

6 SAN JOSE
Grant Ranch County Park

Region: *Santa Clara Valley East*
Total Distance: *16 miles*
Total Elevation Gain: *1900 feet*
Type of Bike: *Mountain Bike*

Ride Rating: *Difficult*
Riding Time: *2-3 hours*
Calories Burned: *1300*
Easy Option: *7 miles*

Terrain

Primarily pasture land for livestock, Grant Ranch County Park is generally very open with little shade, except for some of the trails along the creeks. With a constantly rolling contour, there are some very steep places along the trails. Because the openness can make it quite hot in the summer months, this ride is best done in spring and fall.

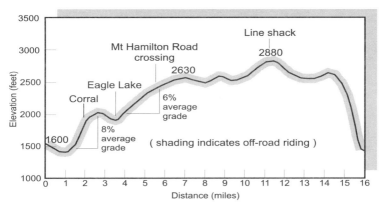

Ride Description

The land now called the Joseph D. Grant Ranch County Park was originally part of the Rancho Cañada de Pala and was a part of a Mexican land grant given to Jose Jesus Bernal in 1839. The property changed hands several times before Joseph D. Grant received it as an inheritance from his father in the latter part of the nineteenth century.

After Joseph's death in 1942, the ranch became the property of his daughter, Josephine. Upon her death in 1972, the ranch was left to the Menninger Foundation and the Save The Redwoods League. Finally, in 1975, Santa Clara County purchased the land for use in its county park system.

Grant Ranch County Park, encompassing some 9,500 acres, is nestled in the foothills of majestic Mt. Hamilton and is populated by both livestock and wildlife. The land is rich with old oaks and is especially beautiful in the springtime when the meadows and slopes are alive with new growth. It is enjoyable other times of the year as well, when the colors take on a golden hue. Panoramic views are numerous, since the park is situated part way up the slopes toward Mt. Hamilton with a base elevation of 1,600 feet.

After a short 1-mile stretch leading away from the main parking area, a rather steep section gets the heart pounding. Once past Eagle Lake, more climbing along Digger Pine Trail and Bohnhoff Trail leads to Mt. Hamilton Road, across which the trail continues. Cañada de Pala Trail leads through a high meadow and to an old line shack formerly used by ranch hands. After this, the rest of the ride is nearly all downhill back to park headquarters.

Almost 2,000 feet of climbing on some rather steep trails make this ride a difficult one. The trails are wide and relatively smooth, so intermediate level skills will get you through.

Starting Point

Grant Ranch County Park is located on Mt. Hamilton Road, east of San Jose. To get there, take the Alum Rock Avenue exit off Highway 680 and proceed east for about 2 miles. Turn right on Mt. Hamilton Road and follow it for about 8 miles to the park. Enter at the main entrance on the right side of the road and go all the way through and to the left where the visitor center and trailhead are located.

Ride Details and Mile Markers

0.0　Proceed EAST from the parking area. Go past two livestock gates to the Hotel Trail.

0.3　bear RIGHT onto Lower Hotel Trail and begin small descent.

1.0　Barn Trail intersection on the right side.

1.6　Livestock gate.

1.8　Continue STRAIGHT through the corral.

1.9　Steep uphill section.

2.3　Trail intersection on the left side.

3.5　Eagle Lake on the right side. Bear LEFT and descend into the canyon. Begin Digger Pine Trail. **EASY OPTION:** Return from this point.

4.6　Turn LEFT onto Bohnhoff Trail and begin a steep climb.

5.5　Continue STRAIGHT across Mt. Hamilton Road and get on Cañada de Pala Trail on the far side.

6.0　Yerba Buena Trail intersection on the left side.

7.3　Continue STRAIGHT at intersection with Los Huecos Trail on the left side.

8.5　Bear LEFT to stay on Cañada de Pala Trail.

10.2 Pass old line shack on the left and bear RIGHT to get on Pala Seca Trail.

12.3 Continue STRAIGHT at the trail intersection to get back on Cañada de Pala Trail.

13.5 Turn RIGHT onto Los Huecos Trail and begin a very steep descent.

14.4 Gate.

15.3 Turn LEFT at the reservoir to stay on trail.

15.6 Continue STRAIGHT through parking lot and turn RIGHT on Mt. Hamilton Road.

16.0 Turn LEFT into park entrance.

16.4 Back at the start point.

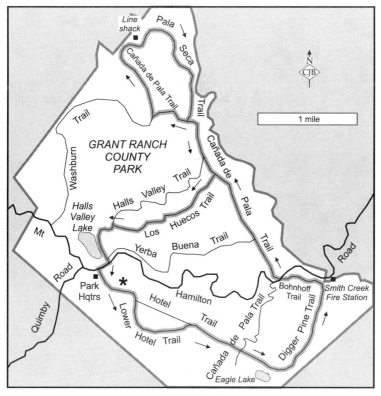

Ride No. 6

Santa Clara Valley: West Foothills

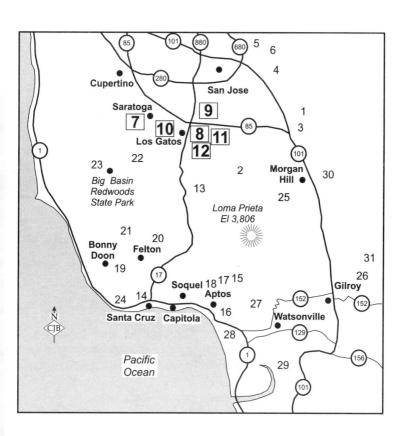

Pacific Ocean

Lick Observatory ⇦

7 SARATOGA

Saratoga and Stevens Canyon Back Roads

Region: Santa Clara Valley West
Total Distance: 14.5 miles
Total Elevation Gain: 1100 feet
Type of Bike: Road Bike

Ride Rating: Moderate
Riding Time: 2 hours
Calories Burned: 600

Terrain

There are two hills to climb, but each of them is fairly modest and the scenery makes them quite worthwhile. Good any time of year, this ride is best in the springtime when the streams are their fullest.

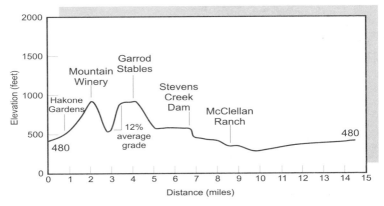

Ride Description

The town of Saratoga serves as the starting point for this ride, which takes you up the hill out of Saratoga and then through wooded country-side, past Stevens Reservoir and then back to Saratoga. In central Saratoga, there are a variety of restaurants, bakeries and shops to enjoy after your ride. In addition, delightful Hakone Gardens is just outside of town and along your route.

Saratoga was originally established by Martin McCarthy in the mid-nineteenth century. Known as McCarthysville until 1863, its name was changed to Saratoga because the presence of the natural springs were reminiscent of those in famous Saratoga Springs, New York.

The first part of the ride entails a rather gentle climb up Big Basin Way out of central Saratoga. On Pierce Road the climb becomes steeper as the route leads you away from busy roads and into the back roads just over the hills. After a steep but short climb up Mt. Eden Road, the route then follows mostly downhill to the Stevens Reservoir and Dam. Past the dam, the route flattens out and winds through peaceful residential neighborhoods as it takes you past historic McCellan Ranch Park and De Anza Community College on the way back to Saratoga.

Starting Point

Start the ride in Saratoga, at the junction of four roads: Saratoga Avenue, Saratoga-Sunnyvale Road, Saratoga-Los Gatos Road (Highway 9), and Big Basin Way (also Highway 9). From Highway 85, take the Saratoga Avenue exit and head west on Saratoga Avenue to Saratoga. Park anywhere convenient near town and start the ride at the intersection.

Ride Details and Mile Markers

0.0   Proceed WEST out of Saratoga on Big Basin Way.

0.8   Hakone Gardens on the left side. Japanese gardens, designed by the former gardener of the Japanese Emperor, contain gazebos and moon bridges. Open to the public with a donation requested.

1.8   Turn RIGHT onto Pierce Road.

2.1   Mountain Winery on the left side. This is the site for the summer concert series, featuring renowned jazz artists in a delightful outdoor setting.

2.8   Turn LEFT onto Mt. Eden Road.

4.1   Garrod Stables on the right side.

5.0   Bear RIGHT onto Stevens Canyon Road.

6.3   Public toilets on the right side and Montebello road just ahead on the left side.

6.8   Stevens Canyon Dam on the right side.

8.1   Turn RIGHT onto McClellan Road.

8.6   Historic McClellan Ranch Park on the left side.

9.5   Highway 85 overcrossing.

9.8   Turn RIGHT onto Stelling Road.

10.2   Highway 85 overcrossing.

11.3   Continue STRAIGHT as Stelling Road becomes Prospect Road.

11.6   Turn RIGHT onto Via Roncole.

11.8   Via Roncole becomes Arroyo de Arguello.

12.4   Turn LEFT onto Wardell Road.

12.7   Turn RIGHT onto Saratoga — Sunnyvale Road.

13.9   Saratoga High School on the left side.

14.6   End back in Saratoga.

Extra Option on Stevens Canyon Road (4 miles out-and-back)

At 5.0 miles, as you would normally leave Mt. Eden Road to bear right onto Stevens Canyon Road, you can instead, turn left onto

Stevens Canyon Road and do an out-and-back to the end of the road. There is a gentle climb along the way, gaining about 600 feet in elevation along the 4 miles to the end. The road is very peaceful and heavily wooded as it follows the route of the creek towards its headwaters.

Extra Option on Montebello Road (5 miles out-and-back)

At the 6.3 mile point is the intersection with Montebello Road. At this point, if you wish to add miles (and about 2,000 feet of climbing), you can proceed up to the end of the paved road and return back to resume the ride. The climb is quite steep at the beginning and then gets less steep as it continues, climbing all the way.

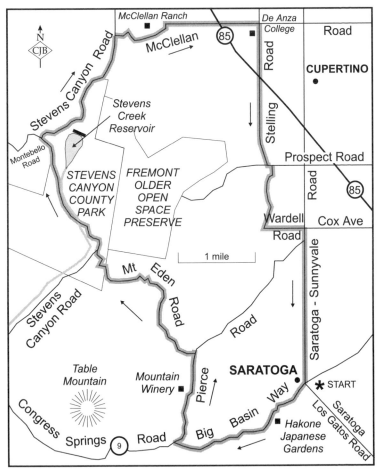

Ride No. 7

8   LOS GATOS
Tour of Los Gatos and Saratoga Foothills

Region: *Santa Clara Valley West*   **Ride Rating:** *Moderate*
Total Distance: *23 miles*   **Riding Time:** *2-3 hours*
Total Elevation Gain: *2400 feet*   **Calories Burned:** *1100*
Type of Bike: *Road Bike*

Terrain

Most of this ride follows along residential streets with very little car traffic. There are some exceptions along busy Saratoga-Los Gatos Road, but there is a wide shoulder suitable for bikes. There are seven distinct hills along the route, making for a good workout with welcome breaks in between the climbs.

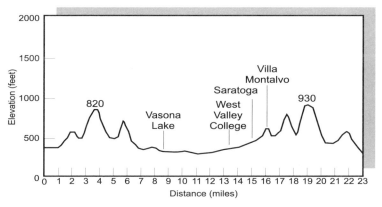

Ride Description

Villa Montalvo, the home of U.S. Senator James D. Phelan, was the site of many lavish parties, during which he entertained many legislators, entertainers, artists and dignitaries, starting around 1914. Upon his death, the estate was left to the San Francisco Art Association with the intention that it be used for the advancement of the arts, especially relating to the development of promising young students. Today there is an art gallery, concert amphitheater, gardens and hiking trails in the hills above the estate, all open to the public.

This ride includes Villa Montalvo in a wide ranging tour of Los Gatos and Saratoga. Starting in Los Gatos, the route takes you east into the country along back roads. After climbing and descending three fairly small hills, the route gets flat as it winds through Vasona Park, a busy place for summer recreation. Following along residential areas through fashionable Saratoga neighborhoods, you will wind your way to the charming town of Saratoga. Just past Saratoga, the hills resume with a climb to Villa Montalvo and then three more hills after that on the way back to Los Gatos.

Starting Point

Start the ride at the corner of University Avenue and Saratoga-Los Gatos Road. To get there, take the Highway 9 (Saratoga-Los Gatos Road) exit off Highway 17 and go west into Los Gatos. Just past University Avenue on the right side is a public parking lot.

Ride Details and Mile Markers

0.0   Proceed SOUTH on University Avenue towards central Los Gatos.

0.5   Turn LEFT onto East Main Street.

0.9   Turn RIGHT onto Alpine Avenue.

1.3   Turn LEFT onto Foster Road.

1.4   Turn RIGHT onto Johnson Avenue.

1.6   Continue STRAIGHT through intersection onto Cypress Way.

1.9   Turn LEFT onto Philips Road.

2.4   Turn RIGHT onto South Kennedy Road and then RIGHT again onto Kennedy Road.

3.8   Crest of the hill on Kennedy Road.

5.0   Turn LEFT onto Shannon Road.

6.8   Bear LEFT at the intersection with Short Road to stay on Shannon Road.

7.6   Continue STRAIGHT across Los Gatos Boulevard onto Roberts Road.

7.9   Turn LEFT onto Blossom Hill Road.

8.0   Highway 17 overpass.

8.1   Turn RIGHT on paved bike path just before main entrance into Vasona County Park. Continue following bike path through the park and along the lake shore. There are restrooms in the park and plenty of places to relax or have a snack.

9.3   Top of the dam.

9.7   Get off the bike path and turn LEFT onto Lark Avenue.

10.0 Turn RIGHT onto Winchester Boulevard and then LEFT onto Wimbledon Drive. Tennis club will then be on the right side.

10.5 Turn LEFT onto Wedgewood Avenue.

11.2 Bear RIGHT to stay on Wedgewood Avenue.

11.5 Turn LEFT onto Pollard Road.

12.1 Turn RIGHT onto Quito Road.

12.4 Turn LEFT onto Allendale Avenue.

13.5 Turn RIGHT just after West Valley College onto Fruitvale Avenue.

13.8   Turn LEFT onto Saratoga Avenue.

15.1   Town of Saratoga. Turn LEFT onto Saratoga-Los Gatos Road.

15.6   Turn RIGHT onto Montalvo Road.

16.3   Villa Montalvo. This is a good place to take a break. There are restrooms and a gift shop for browsing. Continue down the hill when you are ready.

16.7   At the bottom of the hill, turn RIGHT onto Peach Hill Road.

17.5   Turn LEFT onto Glen Una Drive.

17.8   Turn RIGHT to stay on Glen Una Drive.

18.0   Turn RIGHT onto Cañon Road.

19.0   Top of the hill on Cañon Road. Continue STRAIGHT as the road becomes Hidden Drive.

19.9   Turn RIGHT onto Bainter Avenue.

20.2   Turn RIGHT onto Austin Way.

20.4   Turn RIGHT onto Saratoga-Los Gatos Road.

21.2   Turn RIGHT onto Ridgecrest Avenue.

21.8   Turn LEFT onto Beck Avenue.

21.9   Continue STRAIGHT as road becomes Hernandez Road.

22.4   Turn LEFT onto Glen Ridge Avenue.

22.7   Turn RIGHT onto Bachman Avenue and then LEFT onto Massol Avenue.

22.9   Turn RIGHT onto Saratoga-Los Gatos Road.

23.1   Back at the start point.

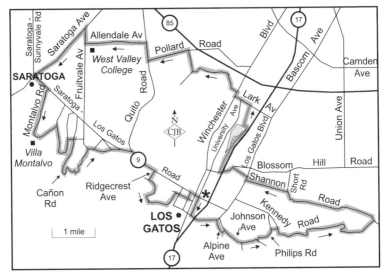

Ride No. 8

Villa Montalvo

9 LOS GATOS
Los Gatos Creek Trail

Region: *Santa Clara Valley West*
Total Distance: *17 miles*
Total Elevation Gain: *400 feet*
Type of Bike: *Road Bike*

Ride Rating: *Easy*
Riding Time: *1-2 hours*
Calories Burned: *300*
Easy Option: *9 flat miles*

Terrain

The Los Gatos Creek Trail is wide and flat with the exception of the final short stretch up to the top of the Lexington Dam. A multi-use trail it is heavily used by runners, walkers, in-line skaters and cyclists, especially on weekends. It is important to be careful and to avoid excessive speed. Although there is little shade along the way, this ride is good any time of year.

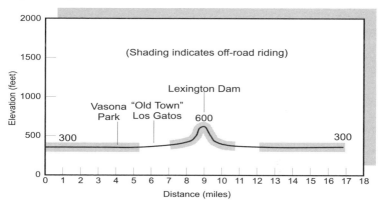

Ride Description

The town of Los Gatos (Spanish for "The Cats") was given its name because the hills above the town were once populated by mountain lions. Today Los Gatos is home to numerous upscale shops and restaurants and its residential neighborhoods are among the most fashionable in the South Bay. Vasona Park, also located in Los Gatos, is the site of a lake for boating and fishing as well as a small-scale children's railroad, the Billy Jones Wildcat Railroad.

The Los Gatos Creek Trail runs along the Los Gatos Creek from its Willow Street terminus in Willow Glen through Vasona Park to Los Gatos and then on to the Lexington Dam and reservoir. This ride is an out-and-back along the trail and starts at the Pruneyard Shopping Center in Campbell. From there, the round trip distance is about 17 miles.

Along the route to Los Gatos, the trail passes several picnic and play areas and goes completely through Vasona Park. Most of the ride is on paved trail, but there may be some places where packed dirt is encountered. A short section follows surface roads into Los Gatos.

Starting Point

The ride starts at the Pruneyard Shopping Center in Campbell. To get there, take the Hamilton Avenue exit from Highway 17 and proceed east on Hamilton Avenue. Turn right on Bascom Avenue and continue for about one half mile to get to the shopping center on the right side at the corner of Campbell Avenue. Park in back, near the access point for the trail.

Ride Details and Mile Markers

0.0 The entry to the bike path is at the north end of the parking area in the rear of the shopping center. Get on the path and proceed SOUTH, toward Los Gatos.

0.3 Bridge under crossing at Campbell Avenue.

1.4 Cross over the bridge to get on the west side of the creek.

1.7 Restrooms on the right side.

1.8 Pond and park on the right side.

2.3 Observation tower on the left side.

3.3 Cross bridge to get back on the east side of the creek. Cross under Lark Avenue.

3.7 Enter Vasona Park. Dam is on the right side.

4.6 Railroad tracks for Billy Jones Wildcat Railroad are to the left. **EASY OPTION:** Return from this point.

4.8 At the trestle, do not cross the bridge, but cross the tracks, instead, and continue on the dirt section of the trail.

5.0 Cross under Blossom Hill Road.

5.2 Get off the trail and turn RIGHT onto Roberts Road. Cross the bridge immediately as the road turns to the right.

5.4 Turn LEFT onto University Avenue.

6.2 Central Los Gatos.

6.3 Turn LEFT onto East Main Street and continue across the bridge over Highway 17. At the far side of the bridge, turn RIGHT to get back on the Los Gatos Creek Trail. This section is a dirt trail, but road bikes will usually be fine.

8.3 End of the trail at Lexington Dam. Return the way you came.

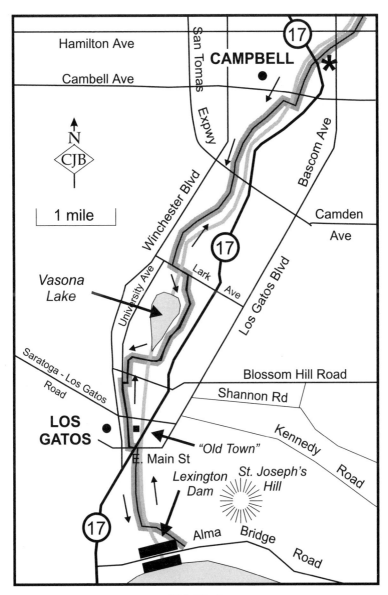

Ride No. 9

10 LOS GATOS
Los Gatos and Castle Rock Loop

Region: *Santa Clara Valley West*   **Ride Rating:** *Difficult*
Total Distance: *36 miles*   **Riding Time:** *3-4 hours*
Total Elevation Gain: *3200 feet*   **Calories Burned:** *1500*
Type of Bike: *Road Bike*

Terrain

There is some car traffic along the early parts of the ride, but there is a wide shoulder for safety. The hill climb is one of the biggest in the South Bay, climbing to an elevation of 3,160 feet at Castle Rock State Park. The last 2 miles of the ride into Los Gatos is along the Los Gatos Creek Trail. This section is a dirt trail, but is usually quite smooth and normally does pose a great problem for road bikes with skinny tires.

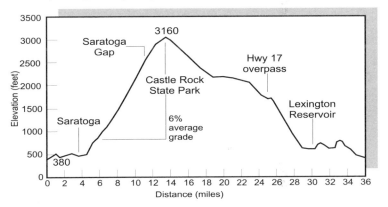

Ride Description

The route leads first from Los Gatos to Saratoga along busy Saratoga-Los Gatos Road. There are usually numerous bikes along this road and there is a wide shoulder. At Saratoga the climb begins. Although not terribly steep, by some standards, the average 6% grade can be quite tiring. At the top of Congress Springs Road is a large rest area, perfect for taking a break before the continuation of the climb along Skyline Boulevard.

At the top of the grade is Castle Rock State Park, the location of a fascinating set of rocks which has been pushed up through the millennia from their previous positions at the bottom of the ocean. Today, the rocks are used for climbers as a means of practicing techniques and honing their skills.

The next 10 miles or so represent perhaps the most delightful stretch of road in the area. Views off to either side can be quite spectacular, especially on a clear day. After crossing Highway 17, the route drops you down through the redwood trees to Lexington Reservoir, follows Alma Bridge Road along the shore to the dam, and then follows Los Gatos Creek Trail for the final return into Los Gatos.

Starting Point

Start the ride at the corner of University Avenue and Saratoga-Los Gatos Road. To get there, take the Highway 9 (Saratoga-Los Gatos Road) exit off Highway 17 and go west into Los Gatos. Just past University Avenue on the right side is a public parking lot.

Ride Details and Mile Markers

0.0   Proceed WEST along Saratoga-Los Gatos Road toward Saratoga. Car traffic is busy along this road.

3.6   Turn LEFT onto Big Basin Way to go into the town of Saratoga. This road become Congress Springs Road when it gets out of town.

4.2   Hakone Gardens on the left side.

5.3   Pierce Road intersection on the right side.

6.0   Intersection with road to Sanborn Skyline County Park on the left side. Continue STRAIGHT ahead.

7.8   Redwood Gulch Road intersection on the right side.

10.9   Turn LEFT onto Skyline Boulevard. There is a major rest area on the left side. This is a good place to take a break, as the climb continues along Skyline Boulevard.

13.6   Castle Rock State Park on the right side. This is the highest point along the route — 3,160 feet.

17.3   Continue STRAIGHT at intersection with Black Road on the left side.

18.9   Continue STRAIGHT at intersection with Gist Road on the left side.

21.1   Turn LEFT onto Bear Creek Road.

21.7   Bear RIGHT onto Summit Road as Bear Creek Road continues straight ahead.

21.9   Bear LEFT to stay on Summit Road. Upper Zayante Road is on the right side.

24.4   Turn LEFT to stay on Summit Road, go down a short and steep section and cross over Highway 17. On the far side of Highway 17, turn LEFT to stay on Summit Road and climb for a short distance.

25.8   Turn LEFT onto Old Santa Cruz Highway.

28.1   Continue STRAIGHT ahead at Holy City.

29.2 Continue STRAIGHT at stop sign and then turn RIGHT just after the stop sign to get on Aldercroft Heights Road. Descend to the reservoir.

30.0 Cross bridge and turn LEFT onto Alma Bridge Road.

34.0 At the dam, turn RIGHT onto the Los Gatos Creek Trail. Follow this trail all the way to its end point at East Main Street

35.5 Turn LEFT onto East Main Street.

35.7 Turn RIGHT onto University Avenue.

36.2 Back at the start point.

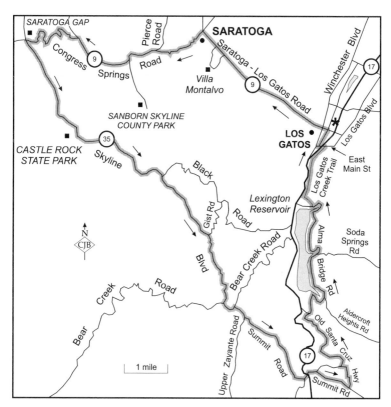

Ride No.10

11   LOS GATOS
Sierra Azul Open Space Preserve

Region: *Santa Clara Valley West*
Total Distance: *16 miles*
Total Elevation Gain: *2800 feet*
Type of Bike: *Mountain Bike*

Ride Rating: *Difficult*
Riding Time: *3-4 hours*
Calories Burned: *1600*

Terrain

The fire roads are generally smooth and wide. There is very little shade, except for some places in the climb and in the final trails leading out of the preserve. There is a lot of climbing and most of it is quite steep. The roads to and from the preserve can sometimes carry substantial car traffic, but the presence of numerous cyclists normally causes the drivers to be careful and courteous.

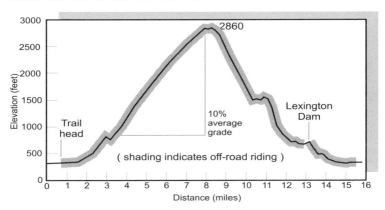

Ride Description

The Sierra Azul (Spanish for "Blue Mountains") Open Space Preserve is a large public-use area stretching from Mount Umunum in the east to Lexington Reservoir in the west. It was acquired and is managed by the Midpeninsula Regional Open Space District (MPROSD) whose headquarters is in Palo Alto. The trails are wide fire roads through the preserve and climb rather steeply to elevations as high as 2,860 feet, offering panoramic views of the Santa Cruz Mountains and the Santa Clara Valley.

This ride is good any time of year, except for when it is cold or windy or after a recent rain. The trail dirt is quite porous, so a light rain is usually absorbed very readily and muddy conditions usually exist only after a hard rainfall. Since there is very little shade, hot summer days might be best to avoid. The mountains are covered with poison oak, so be careful to avoid contact. Bring lots of water, especially when it is hot.

The route takes you along surface roads from the town of Los Gatos to the northern entrance to the preserve on Kennedy Road, up the hill from Los Gatos. From the trailhead on Kennedy Road, you climb steeply and steadily to the high point of the ride at 2,860 feet above sea level. The descent on the far side leads to an exit from the preserve at a trailhead at Lexington Reservoir. A short stretch along Alma Bridge Road along the side of the reservoir will take you to the dam and then to an easy ride back along the Los Gatos Creek Trail. This is a very strenuous ride and includes about 12 miles along the fire roads in the preserve and another 1.8 miles on the Los Gatos Creek Trail. It is intended for the fittest of riders only, although the technical difficulty is not great.

Starting Point

Start the ride at or near Los Gatos High School in Los Gatos. To get there, take the Saratoga Avenue exit (Highway 9) for Los Gatos off Highway 17 (I-880). Travel east on Saratoga Avenue to the intersection with Los Gatos Boulevard. Turn right and proceed on Los Gatos Blvd. (which becomes East Main Street after a short distance) for about ½-mile where the high school will be on the right side. Park anywhere nearby and begin at this point.

Ride Details and Mile Markers

0.0   Proceed EAST on East Main Street (which becomes Los Gatos Blvd.), away from Los Gatos.

0.5   Continue STRAIGHT through the intersection with Saratoga Avenue on the left side.

0.7   Turn RIGHT onto Kennedy Road.

3.0   Summit of Kennedy Road. Trailhead into Sierra Azul is on the right side. There is an information board which may have pertinent messages, so be sure to check it out.

3.6   Steep climbing begins.

6.6   False summit — very steep just ahead.

6.8   First summit (2,560 feet).

6.9   Continue STRAIGHT at the intersection with fire road on the right side.

7.9   First summit (2,560 feet).

8.0   Turn RIGHT at the "tee" and begin descent.

11.0   Four-way trail intersection. Continue STRAIGHT ahead.

11.3   Continue STRAIGHT ahead at the barrier.

12.3   Limekiln Road is visible to the right. Do not try to get over onto it, since it is not the road you want.

12.8 Continue through the gate and turn RIGHT onto the road (Alma Bridge Road).

13.6 Turn RIGHT at the top of the dam to get onto the Los Gatos Creek Trail. Be careful, as there are many usually other trail users.

15.1 Turn RIGHT onto East Main Street at the end of the trail.

15.5 Back at the start point.

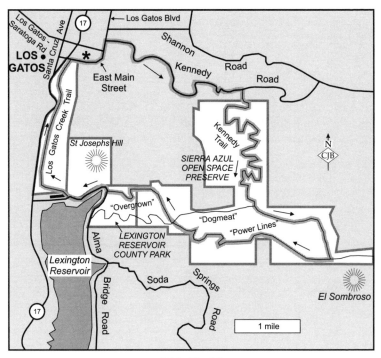

Ride No. 11

12   LOS GATOS
St. Joseph's Hill Open Space Preserve

Region: *Santa Clara Valley West*
Total Distance: *6 miles*
Total Elevation Gain: *900 feet*
Type of Bike: *Mountain Bike*

Ride Rating: *Moderate*
Riding Time: *2 hours*
Calories Burned: *500*
Easy Option: *4 miles*

Terrain

The ride is somewhat steep in places, but is rated moderate because it is not very long and climbs only about 900 feet. Intermediate riders may find it more difficult than they expected because of the grade.

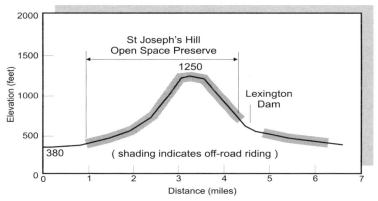

Ride Description

The St. Joseph's Hill Open Space Preserve was acquired from the California Society of the Province of Jesus in 1984 and was subsequently opened for public use. Approximately 170 acres are crossed by the trails, which are generally wide, but include some single track. The remaining 97 acres serve as an easement between the preserve and the Novitiate Winery (now the Mirrasou Cellars). At the top of the hill one can find the remains of the vines used by the original Novitiate when it grew the resident clergy grew their own grapes.

The ride starts in Los Gatos and follows College Avenue and then Jones Road to get to the trailhead. Jones Trail then winds into the preserve and connects with other trails leading to the top of the hill. From the top, the views of Los Gatos beckon the rider to stop for a breather. The ride is good any time of year, but care should be taken since the trails are used by hikers and runners, as well.

Starting Point

The ride starts at or near Los Gatos High School in Los Gatos. To get there, take the Saratoga Avenue exit (Highway 9) for Los Gatos off Highway 17 (I-880). Travel east on Saratoga Avenue to the intersection with Los Gatos Boulevard. Turn right and proceed on Los Gatos Blvd. (which becomes East Main Street after a short distance) for about ½-mile where the high school will be on the right side. Park anywhere nearby and begin the ride at this point.

Ride Details and Mile Markers

0.0   Proceed WEST on East Main Street, toward Los Gatos.

0.2   Turn LEFT onto College Avenue.

0.3   Turn RIGHT to stay on College Avenue.

0.6   Turn RIGHT onto Jones Road.

0.7   Continue STRAIGHT at the gate at the trailhead on Jones Trail. Bear LEFT at the junction as the trail begins. Bikes are not permitted on Flume Trail.

1.1   Trail intersection on the right side.

1.5   Turn LEFT onto Novitiate Trail toward St. Joseph's Hill. **EASY OPTION:** Continue STRAIGHT at this point and jump ahead in the directions to the 3.7 mile point.

1.7   Continue STRAIGHT at the intersection with Manzanita Trail on the right.

1.9   Four trails intersect. Turn RIGHT onto Manzanita Trail (the second trail on the right side).

2.1   Continue STRAIGHT at the intersection with a trail on the right and continue to the top.

2.5   Top of the hill — 1,250 feet. Continue STRAIGHT and begin the downhill towards the dam.

2.6   Trail on the right side.

2.8   Turn LEFT onto Manzanita Trail. Range Trail is to the right.

3.5   Turn LEFT onto Novitiate Trail.

3.7   Turn LEFT onto Jones Trail, heading toward Lexington Reservoir.

4.2   Turn RIGHT after the gate to get on Alma Bridge Road.

4.3   Turn RIGHT just before the dam to get onto Los Gatos Creek Trail.

6.0   Turn RIGHT onto East Main Street at the end of the trail.

6.3   Back at the start point.

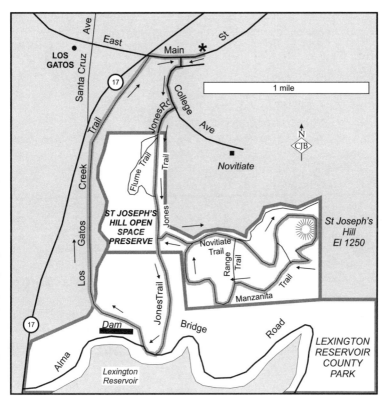

Ride No. 12

Santa Cruz Area: Mountains and Beaches

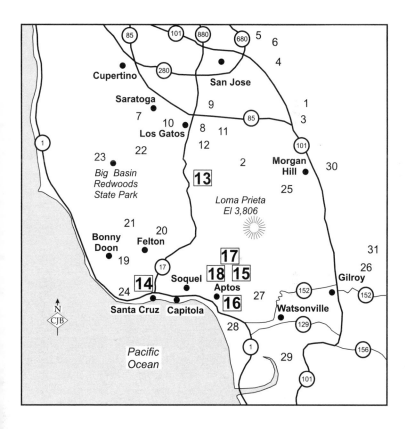

⇦ View from St. Joseph's Hill Open Space Preserve

13   SANTA CRUZ
Los Gatos and Soquel Loop

Region: *Santa Cruz Area*
Total Distance: *50 miles*
Total Elevation Gain: *2700 feet*
Type of Bike: *Road Bike*

Ride Rating: *Difficult*
Riding Time: *5 hours*
Calories Burned: *1600*
Easy Option: *9 miles*

Terrain

This ride has a major hill climb in each direction as it transverses the Santa Cruz Mountains heading from Los Gatos to the coast and then back again. The roads generally carry very little car traffic with the exception of the streets in the vicinity of Santa Cruz and Soquel.

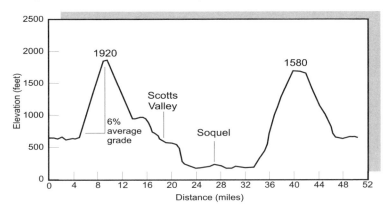

Ride Description

In 1850, an Irishman named Charles McKiernan came to California, ostensibly to make his fortune in the gold rush. He was a little late. Instead of fortune in the Sierra Foothills, he decided on a simpler life, settled in the Santa Cruz Mountains and became a "mountain man". Working at times as a rancher, teamster, road builder and stage operator, he is best known for his chance encounter with a large grizzly bear, at that time common in the mountains above Los Gatos. The grizzly crushed McKiernan's skull in its mighty jaws and only by feigning death did McKiernan survive. The bear left him for dead and McKiernan struggled into town where he was ultimately fitted with a silver plate to fill the gaping hole in his head. Although severely disfigured, he lived for many years and was partly responsible for the building of a stage road through the mountains which today bears his name and is part of the route for this delightful and rather challenging ride.

This ride begins at the Lexington Dam and takes you along the shore of the reservoir and up into the mountains. You will then follow Mountain Charlie Road through the heavily wooded Santa Cruz Mountains, down into Scotts Valley and then on to Santa Cruz. Busy surface streets then lead to Soquel and the return over the hills once again, this time on Soquel-San Jose Road and back to the reservoir and dam.

Starting Point

Start the ride at Lexington Dam, just outside Los Gatos. To get there, take Highway 17 south toward Santa Cruz and get off by turning left onto Alma Bridge Road. There is plenty of parking near the dam.

Ride Details and Mile Markers

0.0   Proceed EAST on Alma Bridge Road, away from Highway 17.

2.9   Soda Springs Road intersection on the left side.

4.4   Turn RIGHT onto Aldercroft Heights Road and begin to climb. **EASY OPTION:** Return from this point.

4.9   Turn LEFT onto Old Santa Cruz Highway.

5.1   Continue STRAIGHT at the intersection with Idylwild Road on the right side.

6.4   Holy City Road on the right side.

7.6   Turn RIGHT onto Mountain Charlie Road. Steeper climb begins.

8.4   Turn RIGHT onto Summit Road and then immediately turn RIGHT again to cross over Highway 17.

8.6   Continue STRAIGHT ahead onto Mountain Charlie Road as Summit Road branches off to the right.

9.5   The site of Mountain Charlie's cabin is on the left side with a historical marker.

13.9   Turn RIGHT onto Glenwood Drive.

14.9   Bean Creek Road intersection on the right side.

16.8   Turn RIGHT onto Scotts Valley Drive.

18.7   Turn LEFT onto Mount Herman Road and then take the first LEFT onto Glen Canyon Road.

19.3   Cross under Highway 17 and then bear RIGHT to stay on Glen Canyon Road.

22.4   Turn RIGHT onto Branciforte Drive.

23.6   Continue STRAIGHT at Goss Avenue as Branciforte Drive becomes Market Street.

23.9   Turn LEFT onto Water Street.

24.5   Turn RIGHT onto Poplar Avenue and then LEFT onto Soquel Avenue.

25.9   Cross Highway 17 and then Soquel Avenue becomes Soquel Drive.

27.6 Turn left onto San Jose-Soquel Road (also called Old San Jose Road).

39.0 Turn LEFT onto Summit Road.

41.8 Turn RIGHT onto Old Santa Cruz Highway.

45.4 Continue STRAIGHT at the intersection with Idylwild Drive on the left.

45.6 Turn RIGHT onto Aldercroft Heights Road and descend to the reservoir.

46.1 Turn LEFT onto Alma Bridge Road.

50.5 End of the ride back at the dam.

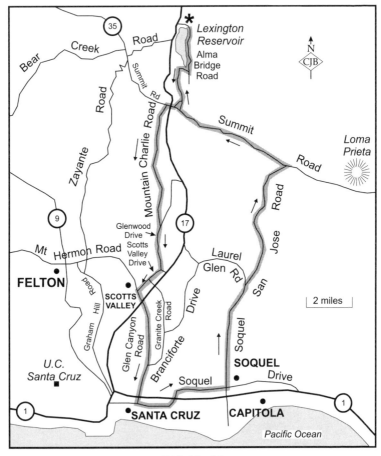

Ride No. 13

14   SANTA CRUZ
Santa Cruz and Capitola Beach Ride

Region: *Santa Cruz Area*   **Ride Rating:** *Easy*
Total Distance: *23 miles*   **Riding Time:** *2-3 hour*
Total Elevation Gain: *200 feet*   **Calories Burned:** *500*
Type of Bike: *Road Bike*   **Easy Option:** *12 flat miles*

Terrain

The roads are quite flat, but there is often substantial car traffic. It is important to be very alert and to stay clear of danger. Bike lanes in many places are provided for extra safety.

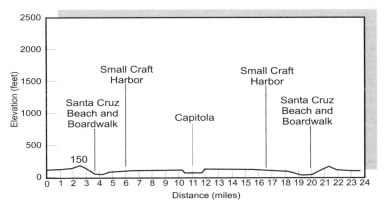

Ride Description

Both Santa Cruz and Capitola have long been immensely popular beach resort towns, enjoyed by outside visitors, local residents and students from nearby U.C. Santa Cruz. This ride follows a leisurely and picturesque route along the shoreline from Natural Bridges State Park, just west of Santa Cruz, to Capitola. It then returns following the same route.

To get the complete experience, expect to spend the better part of a day exploring the many diversions along the way. The ride is good any time of year, but is especially nice on weekdays and during the off-season, when traffic is minimal. Be advised to bring along a jacket or wind-breaker, as the coast can often be quite cool, even when inland temperatures are high.

Starting Point

There is easy parking along the streets just outside of Natural Bridges State Park, near the intersection of Delaware Avenue and Natural Bridges Drive. To get there, take Highway 17 south to Santa Cruz and then follow Highway 1 north out of town. Turn left at the edge of town onto Western Drive. Make an immediate right and then left onto Natural Bridges Drive. Continue to Delaware Street and park anywhere.

Ride Details and Mile Markers

0.0 Go into Natural Bridges State Park through the gate on Delaware Street. Continue all the way through the park to the exit at the far end to get on West Cliff Drive. Be sure to stop at the monarch butterfly sanctuary in the park, especially when the butterflies are in. There is a trail through the area and often thousands of butterflies can be seen in the trees.

0.5 Continue out of the park and get on the bike path along West Cliff Drive.

2.4 Lighthouse and Seal Rock are on the right side.

3.3 Santa Cruz Wharf on the right side. Bikes are permitted to ride out on the wharf.

3.5 Santa Cruz Beach and Boardwalk.

3.9 Go all the way to the end and turn LEFT onto Third Street. Follow this road towards the bridge across the river.

4.3 Turn RIGHT onto Laurel Street, cross the bridge, and turn RIGHT onto the River Levee Bikeway.

4.9 End of the bike path. Turn RIGHT onto East Cliff Drive and climb the small hill.

5.1 Turn RIGHT to stay on East Cliff Drive.

5.4 Museum on the left side.

5.5 Turn RIGHT onto Seabright Avenue, then turn LEFT and follow the path along the edge of the cliff.

5.7 Turn LEFT onto Fourth Avenue and then LEFT again onto Atlantic Avenue.

5.9 Turn RIGHT onto Seabright Avenue.

6.0 Turn RIGHT onto Murray Street.

6.2 Cross the bridge — harbor is on the right side. **EASY OPTION:** Return from this point.

6.3 Turn RIGHT onto Lake Avenue.

6.7 Turn LEFT onto East Cliff Drive and then RIGHT to stay on East Cliff Drive.

7.7 Turn RIGHT to stay on East Cliff Drive.

9.4 Turn RIGHT onto Opal Cliff Drive.

10.1 Turn RIGHT onto Portola Drive.

10.5 Welcome to Capitola.

11.8 Capitola Beach. To return, leave Capitola along Stockton Avenue and retrace your route back to Natural Bridges.

22.0 Back at Natural Bridges State Park.

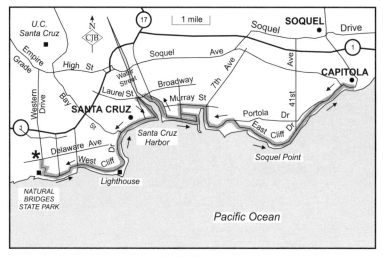

Ride No. 14

Santa Cruz Harbor

15 SOQUEL
Eureka Canyon and Soquel Loop

Region: *Santa Cruz Area*
Total Distance: *40 miles*
Total Elevation Gain: *2700 feet*
Type of Bike: *Road Bike*

Ride Rating: *Difficult*
Riding Time: *4 hours*
Calories Burned: *1600*

Terrain

Although there is usually substantial traffic between Soquel and Corralitos, the wide shoulder will ensure that you have plenty of room. There is a long and steady hill climb with a relatively modest grade on Eureka Canyon Road, followed by a long downhill on smooth and wide Soquel-San Jose Road.

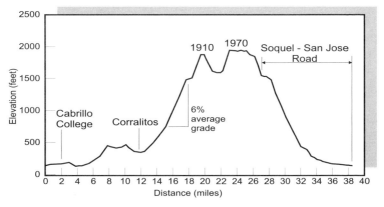

Ride Description

This ride starts in the town of Soquel, just inland from the seaside resort of Capitola. There are several restaurants, antique shops, and a winery (Bargetto Winery) in Soquel for you to enjoy at the conclusion of your ride. This is a difficult ride, with a long uphill climb on Eureka Canyon Road.

The ride starts by heading south and east from Soquel on Soquel Drive. Trout Gulch Road, in Aptos, will get you off busy Soquel Drive and take you along rural roads. Valencia Road and Day Valley Road connect to Freedom Boulevard for the short stretch to Hames Road. Another country road, Hames Road will lead you to the little town of Corralitos.

At Corralitos there is a small country grocery store where you will probably encounter other bicyclists, since it is a major hub for the many beautiful roads around the area favored by local riders. From Corralitos, you will head up Eureka Canyon Road, a steady climb of about 1,700 feet on a reasonably gentle grade. The road starts out going through rustic residential areas, dotted with orchards along the Corralitos Creek, and eventually becomes more lush with redwoods, oaks, and madrone, as it climbs toward the crest.

Along the crest of Eureka Canyon Road, the road gets a bit rougher and presents a slight obstacle along the way. In about 1997, the second of two major mud slides covered the road. This one, unlike the first, which happened several years before and was removed at great cost, remains and may be there for some time. It is necessary to walk and carry your bike around and across the slide, following the path made by other cyclists before you.

The long downhill back to Soquel and along a fairly mild grade and covers a very smooth stretch of road, making it one of the most exhilarating of all downhills in the South Bay.

Starting Point

The town of Soquel is the starting point for the ride. To get there, take Highway 1 south from Santa Cruz and get off at the exit for Capitola and Soquel. Turn left onto Porter Street, passing under the highway. Continue to Soquel Drive, about 0.4 miles away and park somewhere nearby.

Ride Details and Mile Markers

0.0 Proceed SOUTHEAST along Soquel Drive, heading toward Aptos.

2.0 Cabrillo College campus.

3.7 Turn LEFT onto Trout Gulch Road.

4.2 Turn RIGHT onto Valencia Road.

6.7 Turn LEFT onto Day Valley Road.

8.9 Turn LEFT onto Hames Road.

11.0 Turn LEFT onto Eureka Canyon Road at the main intersection in Corralitos. The grocery store is on the right corner, just at the turn. The are rolling hills with only a slight climb for the next two miles.

13.2 Rider Road intersection is on the left.

15.8 Lower Highland Way is on the left.

16.4 Koinonia Conference Grounds on the left.

20.5 False summit — downhill section begins, after which the climb continues.

22.7 Mud slide blocks the road. Carry your bike across.

26.5 Spanish Ranch Road is on the left.

26.8 Crest of the hill at the intersection with Mt. Bache Road on the right. Continue STRAIGHT ahead.

27.9 Skyland Road intersection on the left.

28.2 Turn LEFT onto Soquel-San Jose Road.

36.1 Laurel Glen Road on the right side.

39.5 End of the ride back in Soquel.

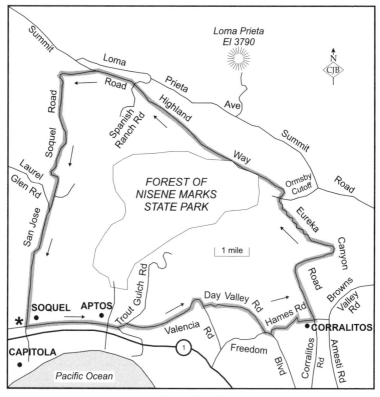

Ride No. 15

16 APTOS

Seacliff Beach and Corralitos Loop

Region: *Santa Cruz Area*
Total Distance: *21 miles*
Total Elevation Gain: *1800 feet*
Type of Bike: *Road Bike*

Ride Rating: *Moderate*
Riding Time: *3 hours*
Calories Burned: *900*
Easy Option: *7 miles*

Terrain

While there are no sustained climbs along this route, there are numerous hills to offer a challenge and a workout to riders of all abilities. The roads are reasonably free of heavy car traffic and offer a wide variety of views of orchards, vineyards and the Pacific Ocean.

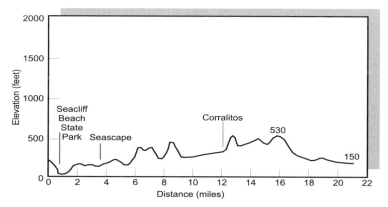

Ride Description

In 1918, a cement ship was built in Oakland for use in World War I as a supply ship. As luck would have it, by the time the *Palo Alto* was completed the war had ended. She languished until 1929, when she was moved to Seacliff Beach in Aptos, was purposely sunk and was outfitted for use as an entertainment spot. She was equipped with a pool, café, and dance hall and was opened for business. The idea never took hold and eventually she was left to withstand the elements on her own. Over the years, the ocean and wind have taken their toll on the ship and today she is battered to a point where it is unsafe to venture about. Most days she is fenced off, but you can still view her at the end of the pier in Seacliff Beach State Park.

The route of this ride begins with a short run down the hill from Aptos to Seacliff Beach, where the pier and the *Palo Alto* can be visited. There is also a fine visitor center where the story of the *Palo Alto* can be seen in vintage photographs and with detailed descriptions. Proceeding on, the route follows pleasantly along the shoreline through the state park and leads to Aptos Beach. From Aptos Beach, you will follow roads toward Seascape, the location of a modern resort on the cliffs above the beach and an upscale residential community. Continuing on after Seascape, the route leads you to the small community of La Selva Beach, where you will then head inland along lightly traveled country roads taking you through eucalyptus trees and fruit orchards to the farming community of Corralitos. From Corralitos, you return to Aptos along more country roads with continuously rolling hills.

Starting Point

Start at the Rancho Del Mar Shopping Center on Soquel Drive in Aptos. To get there, take Highway 1 south from Santa Cruz and get off at the exit for Seacliff Beach and Aptos. Turn left onto State Park Drive and follow it a short distance to Soquel Drive, where the shopping center is on the right. Park in an out-of-the-way spot and begin the ride here.

Ride Details and Mile Markers

0.0 Proceed WEST on State Park Drive, heading toward the beach.

0.3 Cross over Highway 1.

0.6 Continue STRAIGHT into Seacliff Beach State Park. There is no entry fee for bicycles. Turn RIGHT just after the pay station and proceed down the hill toward the beach. At the bottom of the hill, turn LEFT at the visitor center on the left side.

0.7 Seacliff Beach pier on the right side. Feel free to bike onto the pier and to view the cement ship *Palo Alto* at the end of the pier. Continue along the road when you are finished at the pier.

1.0 The road along the beach ends at Aptos Beach and a short pathway begins. Continue along the pathway and ride out into the parking area. At the intersection at the end of the parking area, turn LEFT onto Aptos Beach Drive, heading away from the beach.

1.2 Turn RIGHT to stay on Aptos Beach Drive and climb the hill.

1.8 Turn LEFT onto Rio Del Mar Boulevard and then RIGHT onto Sumner Avenue.

3.6 Turn LEFT onto Seascape Boulevard (Seascape Resort is on the right side facing the ocean.) **EASY OPTION:** Return from this point.

4.3 Turn RIGHT onto San Andreas Road.

5.2 Turn LEFT onto Mar Monte Avenue.

6.1 Cross over Highway 1.

6.5 Turn LEFT onto Larkin Valley Road.

6.9 At the top of the incline, turn RIGHT onto White Road.

8.6 Continue STRAIGHT at the intersection with Calabasas Road on the right side.

9.3 Turn RIGHT onto Freedom Boulevard.

9.7 Corralitos Lagoon visible on the right side.

10.1 Turn LEFT onto Corralitos Road.

12.0 Corralitos Market on the left side. Turn LEFT onto Hames Road.

13.4 Turn RIGHT and then LEFT to stay on Hames Road.

14.1 Turn RIGHT onto Freedom Boulevard and then turn RIGHT almost immediately onto Day Valley Road.

15.4 Turn RIGHT onto Cox Road. Look carefully as this is an easy turn to miss.

17.5 Turn RIGHT onto Valencia Road.

20.1 Continue STRAIGHT onto Trout Gulch Road.

20.5 Turn RIGHT onto Soquel Drive.

21.1 Turn LEFT into the shopping center to get back to the start point.

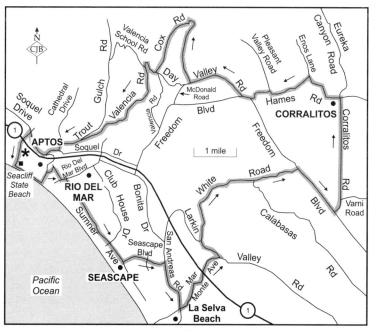

Ride No. 16

17   SOQUEL
Soquel Demonstration Forest

Region: *Santa Cruz Area*
Total Distance: *13 miles*
Total Elevation Gain: *1900 feet*
Type of Bike: *Mountain Bike*

Ride Rating: *Difficult*
Riding Time: *2-3 hours*
Calories Burned: *1100*

Terrain

The trails in Soquel Demonstration Forest offer some of the most technically challenging mountain biking in the South Bay. Although the ride is not particularly long, narrow single-track with steep ups and downs will test the skills of even the most advanced riders.

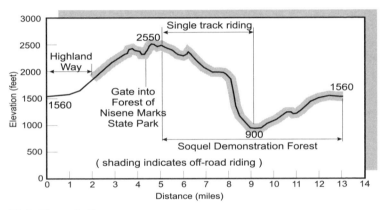

Ride Description

The California Department of Forestry operates "demonstration forests" throughout the state to show how to manage precious timber resources in ways that respect the natural aspects of the forests. At the same time, their management methods provide for the sensible harvesting of lumber, as well as for recreation by the general public. The Soquel Demonstration Forest, located adjacent to The Forest of Nisene Marks State Park, is one recent addition to the system, having been added in 1990.

This ride follows trails through the forest which are particularly unique. While most state parks, county parks and open space preserves forbid bikes from using single-track trails, the Soquel Demonstration Forest does not. Needless to say, rules often change and when you do this ride, be sure to check the information boards within the forest to confirm that these rules still apply. Avoid unmarked trails, they may lead to private property. The legal trails throughout the forest are well marked and easy to follow.

The route starts at the entrance to the park located on Highland Way in the heart of the Santa Cruz Mountains. It initially follows the paved road away from the forest entrance and up the hill toward the rear entrance of the Forest of Nisene Marks State Park. The dirt road into Nisene Marks leads uphill some more before it reaches the trailhead into Soquel Demonstration Forest. From there, single-track trails offer all the challenge you could ask for. Narrow, winding, sometimes overgrown a bit and in many places, steep, the trails lead through the heavy forest, first to an overlook point with sensational views to the west. Steep downhill sections may make it sensible to lower your saddle in order to avoid the dreaded "over-the-handlebar dismount." At the bottom of the hill, the Hihn's Mill Fire Road will take you out of the forest along a steady uphill grade.

Starting Point

To get to the starting point, take Highway 17 south from the Santa Clara Valley and get off at the exit for Summit Road at the top of the grade. Loop around over the highway and continue along Summit Road for about 4 miles to the end of Summit Road. Continue another 5.5 miles after Summit Road changes to Highland Way to get to the forest entrance on the right side. Look closely for it, since it is easy to miss. Park inside the entrance or nearby. The route will bring you out to this point at the end.

Ride Details and Mile Markers

0.0 Proceed SOUTH on Highland Way, up the hill.

0.6 Camp Loma.

2.0 At the top of the grade there is a major intersection. Turn RIGHT onto Buzzard Lagoon Road. This is a dirt road that leads into The Forest of Nisene Marks State Park.

2.4 Gate on the right side. This is private property, so do not enter here.

2.5 Continue STRAIGHT through gate.

2.9 Turn RIGHT onto unmarked Aptos Creek Fire Road (Buzzard Lagoon Road continues straight ahead).

3.5 First of several unmarked trails on the right. Do not enter.

4.3 Continue STRAIGHT past the gate into The Forest of Nisene Marks State Park.

5.2 Turn RIGHT off the fire road into the Soquel Demonstration Forest. Look for the information board and well-marked trail signs. Get on Ridge Trail. Prepare for the single-track.

5.9 Bear LEFT to stay on Ridge Trail. Corral Trail goes to the right.

6.8 Turn LEFT to stay on Ridge Trail where Sulphur Springs Trail continues straight ahead.

7.4 Overlook on the left side. This is a good place to take a breather and enjoy the views to the coast.

7.8 Turn RIGHT onto Tractor Trail. Ridge Trail continues straight ahead. Prepare for steep descent where is may be best to walk.

9.3 Turn RIGHT onto Hihn's Mill Road, a wide fire road.

10.6 Continue STRAIGHT at the intersection with Sulphur Springs Trail on the right side.

13.0 Continue STRAIGHT past the gate to leave the forest.

13.2 End of the ride back on Highland Way.

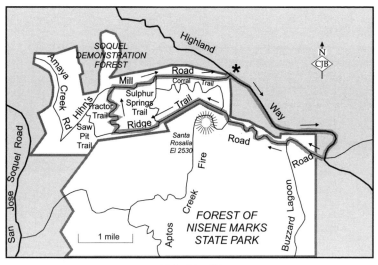

Ride No. 17

18   APTOS
The Forest of Nisene Marks and Sand Point Overlook

Region: *Santa Cruz Area*
Total Distance: *17 miles*
Total Elevation Gain: *1500 feet*
Type of Bike: *Mountain Bike*

Ride Rating: *Moderate*
Riding Time: *3 hours*
Calories Burned: *1100*
Easy Option: *9 miles*

Terrain

This out-and-back ride follows into the park along a paved road at first and then along a wide and smooth fire road. Majestic redwoods line the roads all the way, providing ample shade for even the hottest summer days. The steep part of the hill only begins at about the 4-mile point, so this ride is can also be made quite easy simply by turning around before the hill climb.

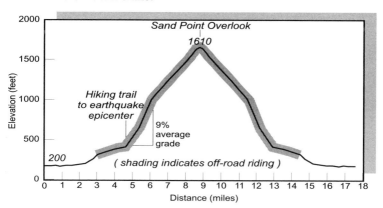

Ride Description

The Forest of Nisene Marks State Park is located on property once owned by the Loma Prieta Lumber Company and was logged extensively in the early part of the twentieth century. In the 1950s, the Marks family purchased the property and halted logging operations to save the remaining redwoods. In 1963, the property was given to the state of California by the Marks children in memory of their mother, Nisene, with the stipulation that the park be operated as a semi-wilderness, without major improvements. As a result, there is neither a visitor center nor a ranger station and the facilities are somewhat spare.

This ride will take you into the park along the main fire road. The route leads to the spot which was formerly believed to be the epicenter of the Loma Prieta Earthquake of 1989. Later analysis revealed, however, that the epicenter was actually some distance away. You can get there by taking the Aptos Creek Trail, but you may not take bikes along that trail. If you intend to hike to the epicenter, be sure to bring along a bike lock and suitable shoes, as the hike is about 1 mile down the trail.

Continuing past this trailhead along the fire road, the grade quickly becomes quite steep and finally leads to the Sand Point Overlook, a flat spot with views to the coast. The return is back the way you came.

Starting Point

To get to the starting point, take Highway 1 south from Santa Cruz. Get off in Aptos at the exit for Seacliff Beach-Aptos and turn left onto State Park Drive. Turn right onto Soquel Drive and follow it under the railroad bridge. Bear left and then look for the small road on the left side. Park somewhere nearby and begin the ride here.

Ride Details and Mile Markers

0.0 Proceed NORTH away from Soquel Drive along Aptos Creek Road.

1.8 Picnic area on the right side.

1.9 Cross over a bridge.

2.9 Porter family picnic area — continue STRAIGHT past the gate onto Aptos Creek Fire Road.

3.2 Cross Aptos Creek.

3.5 Loma Prieta Mill site on the left side.

4.4 Cross bridge over the creek.

4.5 Trailhead for Aptos Creek Trail on the right side. The earthquake epicenter is down this trail about 1 mile. **EASY OPTION:** Return from this point.

4.6 Aptos Creek Fire Road begins to climb very steeply.

8.8 Sand Point Overlook with views toward the ocean. Reverse yourself at this point and return the way you came.

17.6 Back at the start point.

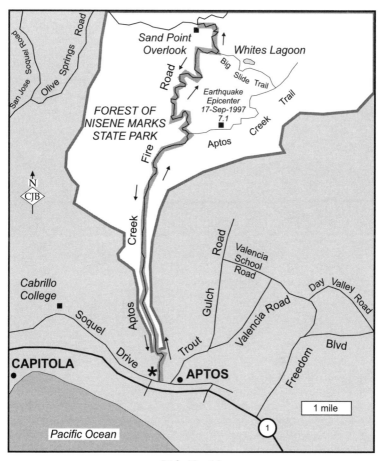

Ride No. 18

West Santa Cruz Area: Mountains and Forests

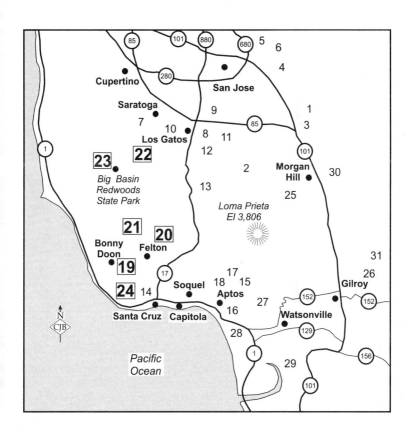

⇦ The forest of Nisene Marks State Park

19 SANTA CRUZ
Empire Grade and Bonny Doon

Region: *West Santa Cruz Area*
Total Distance: *27 miles*
Total Elevation Gain: *2000 feet*
Type of Bike: *Road Bike*

Ride Rating: *Difficult*
Riding Time: *3 hours*
Calories Burned: *1100*

Terrain

The hill climbs are on smooth roads with relatively moderate steepness, but the climbs are sustained over long distances.

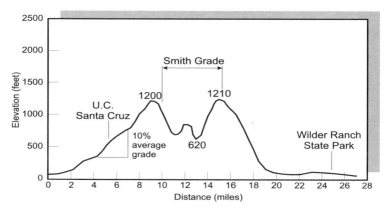

Ride Description

The campus of the University of California at Santa Cruz is one of the highlights of this ride. It is situated on land which was formerly owned by Henry Cowell, who operated a lime and cement company and also had an operating ranch on it. A 2,000-acre parcel of the property was sold to the University of California system in 1961. The campus architecture has been designed to blend in with the natural environment of the site. Some of the original ranch buildings have been restored and are plainly visible as your tour the campus.

The route of this ride begins at Natural Bridges State Park and initially follows the scenic coastline along West Cliff Drive. It leads up to the campus and then along Empire Grade up a long hill climb. Smith Grade will drop you down through some pristine forests and then back up again to Bonny Doon, a small community nestled in the woods. Bonny Doon Road will provide an exhilarating descent to Highway 1 for the return to Santa Cruz.

Starting Point

Plenty of free parking is available along the streets near the rear entrance to Natural Bridges State Park, close to the intersection of Natural Bridges Road and Delaware Avenue. To get there, take Highway 1 north out of Santa Cruz and turn left at Western Drive. Make an immediate right onto Mission Street and then left onto Natural Bridges Road. Continue to the intersection with Delaware Avenue.

Ride Details and Mile Markers

0.0   Go into Natural Bridges State Park through the gate on Delaware Street. Continue all the way through the park to the exit at the far end to get on West Cliff Drive. Be sure to stop at the monarch butterfly sanctuary in the park, especially when the butterflies are in. There is a trail through the area and often thousands of butterflies can be seen in the trees.

0.5   Continue out of the park and get on the bike path along West Cliff Drive.

2.4   Lighthouse and Seal Rock are on the right side.

3.1   Turn LEFT onto Bay Street.

4.1   Turn LEFT at High Street. High Street becomes Empire Grade.

5.1   Lighthouse and Seal Rock are on the right side.

5.8   U.C. Santa Cruz campus is to the right.

10.1   Turn LEFT onto Smith Grade.

10.4   Steep downhill begins.

12.1   Climb for about 1 mile.

15.3   Turn LEFT onto Bonny Doon Road — downhill all the way to the coast.

18.6   Turn LEFT onto busy Highway (Pacific Coast Highway). Be very careful — walk your bike across the road.

25.1   Wilder Ranch State Cultural Preserve on the right side.

26.6   Turn RIGHT onto Shaffer Road, then LEFT onto Mission Street.

26.9   Turn RIGHT onto Natural Bridges Road.

27.2   Back at the start point.

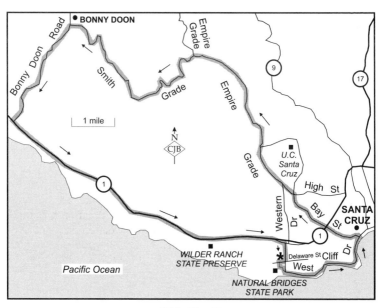

Ride No. 19

Historic Buildings on U.C. Santa Cruz campus

20 FELTON
Zayante Road and Bear Creek Road Loop

Region: *Santa Cruz Area* **Ride Rating:** *Difficult*
Total Distance: *28 miles* **Riding Time:** *3 hours*
Total Elevation Gain: *2500 feet* **Calories Burned:** *1200*
Type of Bike: *Road Bike*

Terrain

Quiet mountain roads characterize much of this ride. The last part of the route requires some time on busy Highway 9 between Boulder Creek and Felton, but this part can usually be done fast since it is mainly downhill and drivers usually have plenty of time to see cyclists ahead. There is usually plenty of shade along the route, so the ride can be quite comfortable, even in the summer.

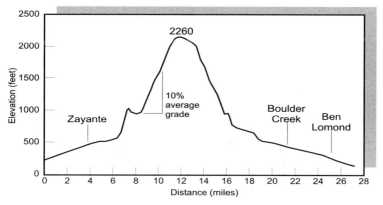

Ride Description

This loop ride follows some remote roads through lush redwood forest on the western slope of the Santa Cruz Mountains. Beginning in Felton, the route goes along an old railroad grade, at one time used for carrying the timber from logging areas to the mills. Continuing through the tiny hamlet of Zayante, the roads will begin to climb, at some times becoming somewhat steep. Along the ridge of the mountains at the top, views to the coast present themselves. An exhilarating downhill into Boulder Creek along Bear Creek Road is the reward for the hard climb. The final stretch back to Felton is along busy Highway 9.

Starting Point

Start the ride at or near a shopping center in Felton. To get there, take Highway 17 south toward Santa Cruz. Get off at Mount Herman

Road and proceed west to Felton. Turn left onto Graham Hill Road and park in the shopping center on the left side.

Ride Details and Mile Markers

0.0   Proceed EAST along Graham Hill Road.
0.2   Intersection with Conference Drive is on the left.
0.3   Turn LEFT onto Zayante Road.
2.2   Intersection with Quail Hollow Road is on the left.
2.9   Intersection with Lompico Road is on the left.
3.9   Pass through Zayante.
11.0   Turn LEFT onto Summit Road.
11.2   Bear LEFT to get on Bear Creek Road.
11.9   Bear LEFT to stay on Bear Creek Road-Skyline Boulevard is on the right.
21.2   Turn LEFT onto Highway and head toward Boulder Creek.
21.4   Continue through Boulder Creek.
23.1   Continue through Brookdale.
24.9   Continue through Ben Lomond.
27.9   Turn LEFT onto Graham Hill Road in Felton.
28.0   Back at the start point.

Vineyards along Bear Creek Road

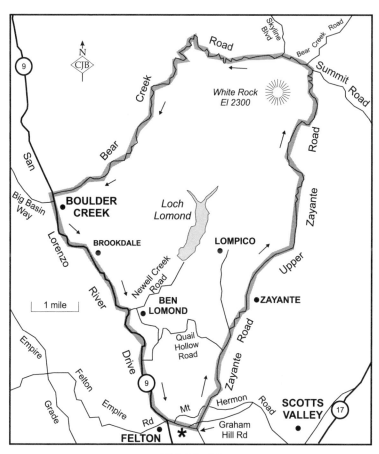

Ride No. 20

21 FELTON
Felton Empire Road

Region: *West Santa Cruz Area*
Total Distance: *30 miles*
Total Elevation Gain: *2800 feet*
Type of Bike: *Road Bike*

Ride Rating: *Difficult*
Riding Time: *4 hours*
Calories Burned: *1400*
Easy Option: *13 miles*

Terrain

This ride follows mostly shady roads through the lush redwood forests so characteristic of the Santa Cruz Mountains. Most of the time there is little car traffic. The exception is the stretch at the end of the ride along Highway 9 from Boulder Creek to Felton. Since it is generally downhill along this road, it is fairly easy to stay safely in view of approaching motorists. There is one big hill climb along Felton Empire Road and then continuing along Empire Grade.

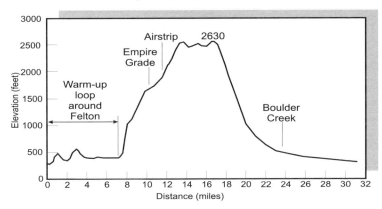

Ride Description

Beginning in Felton, a former lumber town nestled in the lush Santa Cruz Mountains, this route will take you first along Zayante Road, following along the now-idle railroad tracks formerly used for hauling lumber to the mills. Branching off onto Quail Hollow Road, the rolling terrain serves as an excellent warm-up for the hill climb ahead. Completing the circle around Felton, the route then leads steadily up along Felton Empire Road through the dense forests. At the top of Felton Empire Road, you will continue climbing on Empire Grade Road to the intersection with Jamison Road. A very steep and winding descent along Jamison Road will test your wrist muscles as you need to be continually on the brakes to control your speed. At the bottom of the hill, you will then follow busy Highway 236 into Boulder Creek, a good place to take a break. The final section of the route follows along Highway 9 back to Felton.

Starting Point

Start the ride at or near a shopping center in Felton. To get there, take Highway 17 south toward Santa Cruz. Get off at Mount Herman Road and proceed west to Felton. Turn left onto Graham Hill Road and park in the shopping center on the left side.

Ride Details and Mile Markers

0.0   Proceed EAST along Graham Hill Road.

0.2   Intersection with Conference Drive is on the left.

0.3   Turn LEFT onto Zayante Road.

2.2   Turn LEFT onto Quail Hollow Road.

4.3   Turn LEFT onto Glen Arbor Road.

4.9   Turn LEFT onto Highway 9, back toward Felton.

6.6   Back in Felton. Turn RIGHT onto Felton Empire Road and begin climbing. **EASY OPTION:** Turn LEFT to return to the start point.

9.5   Undeveloped Cowell Redwoods State Park is on the right side.

10.3   Turn RIGHT onto Empire Grade and continue climbing.

11.3   Landing strip on the left side.

12.1   Pine Flat Road intersection of the left side.

14.1   Alba Road intersection on the right side.

16.6   Camp Lomond (California Youth Authority) is on the left side.

18.1   Turn RIGHT onto Jamison Road and begin very steep descent.

21.0   Turn RIGHT onto Highway 236 to head toward Boulder Creek.

23.7   Turn RIGHT onto Highway 9. Pass through Boulder Creek center.

25.5   Brookdale.

27.0   Ben Lomond.

30.2   Back in Felton. Turn LEFT Graham Hill Road.

30.4   Back at the start point.

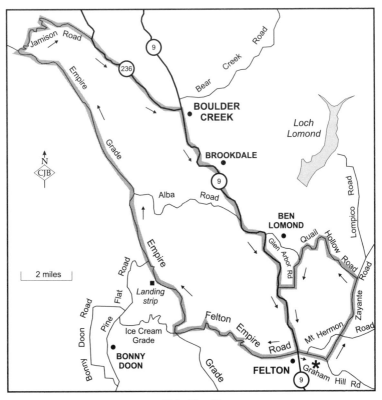

Ride No. 21

22   **SARATOGA**
Big Basin and Castle Rock Loop

Region: *West Santa Cruz Area*
Total Distance: *43 miles*
Total Elevation Gain: *4300 feet*
Type of Bike: *Road Bike*

Ride Rating: *Difficult*
Riding Time: *5 hours*
Calories Burned: *2000*

Terrain

This loop is quite hilly and is only for those who like the rigorous workout associated with extended climbing. It follows along well-paved roads which often have significant car traffic on summer weekends. The stretch of road into Big Basin is quite narrow and requires extra caution.

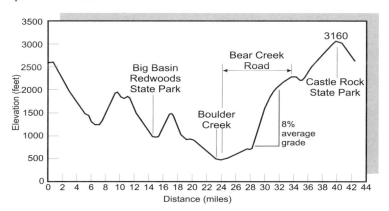

Ride Description

One of the finest overnight hikes in the entire Bay Area is along the well-traveled Skyline-to-the-Sea Trail in the Santa Cruz Mountains. Beginning at Castle Rock State Park on Skyline Boulevard above Saratoga, the trail takes intrepid backpackers down through lush redwood forests and goes completely through Big Basin State Park. It terminates at the ocean at Waddell Beach, north of Santa Cruz. This ride leads along roads through the mountains and parallels the Skyline-to-the-Sea Trail for several miles in the beginning. There are numerous places where close observation will reveal trail heads on either side of the road.

Beginning at Saratoga Gap, high above Saratoga, the route will lead you along some of the most scenic of all the roads in the mountains. You initially descend to Waterman's Gap, at which point you branch off onto Highway 236 for the narrow road leading to Big Basin State

Park. After Big Basin, the route continues generally downhill to the mountain town of Boulder Creek, the last place where services are available. From there, the climb back up the hills to Skyline Boulevard is quite steep in some places. Along Skyline Boulevard at the top of the climb is Castle Rock State Park, the site of some very unusual rock formations highly favored by climbers for their convenience and uniqueness.

Starting Point

Start the ride at a parking area at the intersection of Highway 9 (Congress Springs Road) and Skyline Boulevard. Known as Saratoga Gap, this place is a common meeting spot for mountain bikers who ride the trails just to the north. To get there, take Highway 85 and get off at the exit for Saratoga Avenue. Follow Saratoga Avenue west to the town of Saratoga. Follow Big Basin Way through town and up the hill to Saratoga Gap. The road changes its name along the way.

Ride Details and Mile Markers

0.0   Proceed WEST along Highway 9 toward Big Basin.

6.0   Bear RIGHT to get on Highway 236 continuing towards Big Basin.

10.8   Use caution around the hairpin turn.

14.0   Big Basin State Park. Restrooms and a grocery store are available.

19.9   Golf course on the left side.

23.3   Boulder Creek — turn LEFT onto Highway 9.

23.6   Turn RIGHT onto Bear Creek Road.

27.8   Begin climbing steeply.

32.7   Turn LEFT onto Skyline Boulevard.

35.0   Gist Road intersection is on the right side.

36.6   Black Road intersection is on the right side.

40.0   Castle Rock State Park is on the left side. There are restrooms but no water is available.

43.0   Back at the start point at Saratoga Gap.

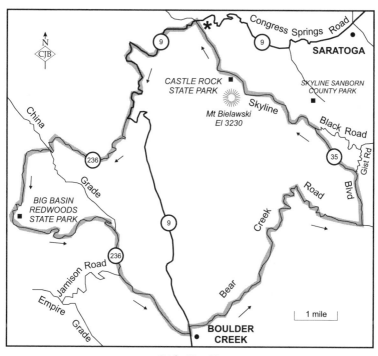

Ride No. 22

Big Basin Redwoods State Park

23 BIG BASIN
Big Basin Redwoods State Park

Region: *West Santa Cruz Area*
Total Distance: *16 miles*
Total Elevation Gain: *2000 feet*
Type of Bike: *Mountain Bike*

Ride Rating: *Moderate*
Riding Time: *3 hours*
Calories Burned: *1300*

Terrain

The ride through Big Basin Redwoods State Park is along wide fire roads with some bumps but no technically difficult sections. There is plenty of climbing, but the presence of much shade along the way makes this ride comfortable even on hot summer days.

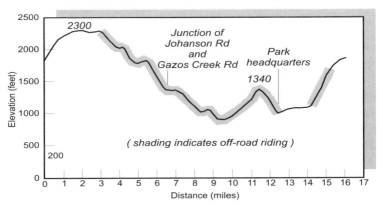

Ride Description

Big Basin State Park is the home of some of the most majestic redwoods in the state and has long been enjoyed by South Bay Area residents for its extensive hiking, camping, and picnicking. The 15,000-acre park is located on the western slope of the Santa Cruz Mountains and extends all the way to the sea, at Waddell Creek. Logging was done here until 1902, when the area was established as the California Redwoods Park. Today you can see the stumps of many of the original redwoods surrounded by second-growth trees which are rapidly reclaiming the forest.

This ride takes you nearly completely around the eastern part of the park. You start about 3 miles northeast of the park headquarters and begin by climbing up China Grade, a paved road, to get to Middle Ridge Fire Road, at a rear entrance into the park. After a short distance on Middle Ridge Fire Road, you branch off and head west along Johansen Road, going mostly downhill along the bumpy, but wide fire road. At the main junction, the route then takes you left and then left again to continue down and then to climb back out towards park headquarters along Gazos Creek Fire Road. Once at the center of the park, you can stop and get refreshments at the store and check out the informative visitor center there. The route then follows along the paved roadway through the picnic areas of the park to get to the final climb back to where you started.

Starting Point

Big Basin Redwoods State Park is located up and over the hill from Saratoga. To get there, take the Saratoga Avenue exit off Highway 85 and head west toward Saratoga. Continue through Saratoga on Big Basin Way and follow this road up the mountain to Skyline Boulevard. Continue across Skyline Boulevard for about 6 miles to the intersection with Highway 236. Turn right on Highway 236 toward Big Basin and proceed for about 5 miles to the intersection with China Grade. Park near this intersection to begin the ride.

Ride Details and Mile Markers

0.0   Begin the ride by going up the hill along China Grade.

2.4   Continue STRAIGHT at the intersection with a road on the right. Dirt road begins here.

3.3   Turn LEFT into Big Basin. Continue past the gate on Middle Ridge Fire Road.

4.1   Turn RIGHT onto Johansen Road.

6.5   At the main fire road junction, turn LEFT onto Gazos Creek Road.

6.6   Turn LEFT again to stay on Gazos Creek Road.

9.2   Lowest point along the ride. Begin climbing.

11.5   Continue STRAIGHT at the intersection with Middle Ridge Fire Road on the right.

11.6   Continue STRAIGHT at the intersection with Middle Ridge Fire Road on the left.

12.6   Turn LEFT onto North Escape Road, a paved road in the central part of the park. To go to the park headquarters and store, turn right here and follow the road about a mile, then return back to resume the ride here.

14.3   Begin the dirt section of the road here and begin climbing out to the road.

15.1   Turn LEFT onto the paved road, Big Basin Highway.

16.1   Back at the start point.

Extra Option to Overlook (4 miles each way)

There is an extra option at the 11.5-mile point. This option will take you about 2 miles uphill with an elevation gain of about 400 feet to an overlook point. At the overlook, you will get a panoramic view of the entire Waddell Creek Basin, extending all the way to the ocean, about 5 miles distant. To ride this option turn right onto Middle Ridge Fire Road and follow it to Hihn Hammond Road. Continue along Hihn Hammond Road to the overlook, at which point there is a bench for sitting. Return the way you came to resume the ride.

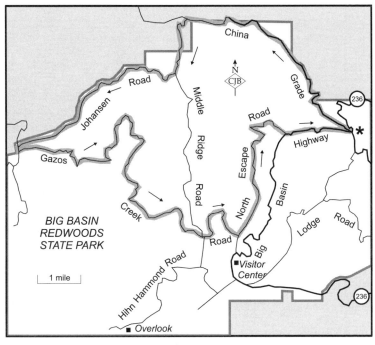

Ride No. 23

24   SANTA CRUZ
Wilder Ranch State Historic Preserve

Region: *West Santa Cruz Area*
Total Distance: *18 miles*
Total Elevation Gain: *1800 feet*
Type of Bike: *Mountain Bike*

Ride Rating: *Moderate*
Riding Time: *3 hours*
Calories Burned: *1200*
Easy Option: *3 flat miles*

Terrain

The terrain of this ride offers variety and challenge for even the most skilled mountain bikers. There is much single-track and plenty of steepness. Expect to push your bike up some sections.

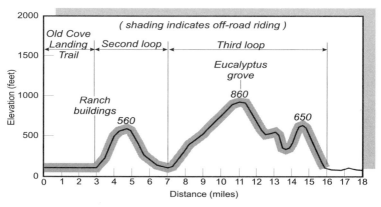

Ride Description

Single-track trail through forests and meadows, numerous stream crossings, and a spectacular ride along the cliffs at the edge of the ocean give Wilder Ranch a variety rarely found in mountain biking. Formerly an operating ranch, it is now a cultural preserve, only recently opened to the public.

The ride is divided into three distinct loops, each starting from very near the park headquarters. In this way, the ride can be tailored to any particular need. The first loop, 3 miles in length, is the easiest. Totally flat, it takes you out away from the park headquarters and follows Old Cove Landing Trail along the edge of the shoreline before returning back to the starting point. You definitely will not want to miss this section for the sheer beauty of the coastline.

The second loop takes you through the ranch compound where you can explore the old buildings. It then heads inland and uphill along a narrow single-track trail with several stream crossings along the way before returning down a wide fire road.

The third and final loop is the longest. It leads along ridges and then through a meadow, finally passing through a eucalyptus grove at its highest point. The return has several more stream crossings and then passes through a heavy forest before coming out onto the main road, Highway 1. The return to park headquarters is along busy Highway 1, but a wide shoulder makes it quite safe.

Starting Point

Wilder Ranch is located on Highway 1, about 2 miles north of Santa Cruz. There is a modest day use fee for cars that can be avoided by parking along the main road and riding in.

Ride Details and Mile Markers

- 0.0 Proceed out of the parking area onto Old Cove Landing Trail.
- 2.1 Continue STRAIGHT toward park headquarters where the trail becomes a dirt road.
- 2.5 Back at the parking area where you began, proceed down the paved road toward the Cultural Preserve. **EASY OPTION:** The ride ends here.
- 2.6 Turn LEFT to go through the ranch compound. Continue on the trail through the tunnel which passes under Highway 1.

Along Old Cove Landing Trail

3.1 Continue STRAIGHT at the trail intersection on the left side, then bear LEFT at the main trail junction to get on Wagon Wheel Trail.

4.7 Continue STRAIGHT at trail intersection on the right side.

4.9 Begin descent back to the main trail junction.

6.9 Proceed STRAIGHT through the main trail junction and turn RIGHT onto Wilder Ranch Loop Trail.

7.7 Single-track trail intersection on the left side.

8.4 Bear RIGHT onto single-track Twin Oaks Trail.

9.6 At the 4-way trail junction, proceed through and bear RIGHT to head uphill toward the eucalyptus grove.

10.8 Continue STRAIGHT through the eucalyptus grove at the top of the hill.

12.8 Continue STRAIGHT at the trail intersection on the left.

13.0 Back at the 4-way trail junction, turn LEFT and then RIGHT onto the Enchanted Loop Trail.

13.8 Continue STRAIGHT at the trail intersection on the right.

14.4 Turn RIGHT sharply onto Wilder Ridge Loop Trail, heading downhill towards Highway 1.

15.9 Turn LEFT onto Highway 1.

17.8 Turn RIGHT into Wilder Ranch Preserve.

18.0 Back at the start point.

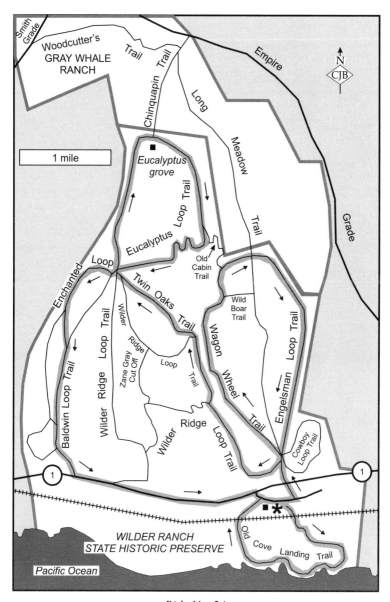

Ride No. 24

South County:
Ranches and Farms

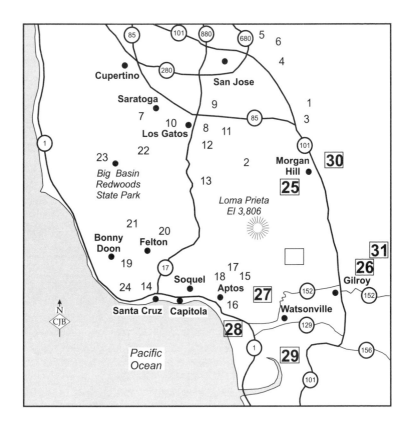

25 MORGAN HILL
Chesbro and Uvas Reservoirs

Region: *South County*
Total Distance: *19 miles*
Total Elevation Gain: *700 feet*
Type of Bike: *Road Bike*

Ride Rating: *Easy*
Riding Time: *2 hours*
Calories Burned: *400*

Terrain

Although the terrain is rolling, there are no serious hills along the route and the roads usually carry very little car traffic. There are no services along the route, so be sure to carry all the water and snacks you need.

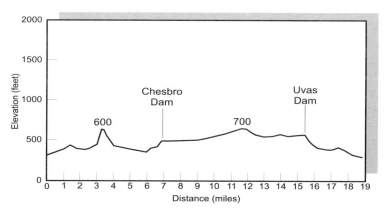

Ride Description

Popular opinion has it that the town of Morgan Hill is named for the prominent peak nearby. That peak is actually named El Toro and the town name comes from a completely different source.

Martin Murphy was the patriarch of a large Irish family that settled in this area around 1844. His son, Daniel Murphy, eventually came to own a vast amount of land, some 10,000 acres, in all. Daniel's land manager and brother-in-law, one Hiram Morgan Hill, was very influential in local affairs and supplied the town with its eventual name, Morgan Hill.

The route of this ride will take you along rural country roads as it circles the two major water sources for the Morgan Hill area, Chesbro and Uvas (Spanish for "grapes") Reservoirs. The ride is good any time of year, but is best in the springtime and early summer, when the hillsides are alive with new growth and the streams are running with the runoff from winter rains.

Starting Point

Start the ride at a small park along Edmundson Avenue in Morgan Hill. To get there, take Highway 101 south from San Jose and get off at the exit for Tennant Avenue. Follow Tennant Avenue west to Monterey Road, and turn right onto Monterey Road for a short distance. Turn left onto Edmundson Avenue and proceed less than ½-mile to the park entrance on the right side.

Ride Details and Mile Markers

0.0   Proceed WEST along Edmundson Avenue, heading slightly uphill away from Monterey Road.

1.5   Turn LEFT onto Oak Glen Avenue.

2.5   Turn RIGHT onto Sycamore Avenue.

3.3   Top of the hill.

4.5   Turn RIGHT onto busy Watsonville Road.

5.2   Turn RIGHT onto Uvas Road.

5.8   Narrow bridge over Uvas Creek. Begin heading uphill toward the first dam.

7.0   Uvas Dam and reservoir on the right side.

7.5   Toilets on the right side.

11.0   Croy Road intersection on the left side.

11.8   Top of the hill.

12.7   Turn RIGHT onto Oak Glen Avenue.

13.2   Chesbro Reservoir visible on the right side.

14.5   Willow Springs Road intersection on the left side.

15.5   Chesbro Dam on the right side.

15.8   Turn RIGHT to stay on Oak Glen Avenue. Llagas Road is to the left.

17.5   Turn LEFT onto Edmondson Avenue.

19.0   Back at the start point.

Extra Option on Croy Road (4 miles out-and-back)

At the 11.0 mile point is the intersection with Croy Road. Uvas Canyon County Park is at the end of Croy Road, about 4 miles distant. Hiking trails and a picnic area are available at the park. Bikes are not permitted on the trails. The ride to the park is slightly uphill along a lightly traveled rural road. There is no other outlet, so you must return back out the way you went in.

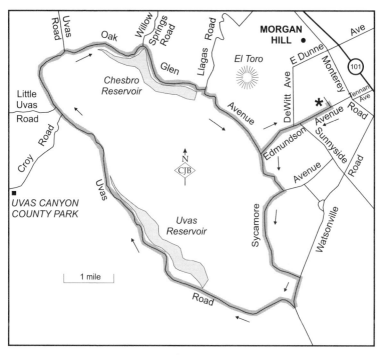

Ride No. 25

South County scene

26   GILROY
Gilroy Hot Springs and Cañada Road

Region: *South County*
Total Distance: *23 miles*
Total Elevation Gain: *1000 feet*
Type of Bike: *Road Bike*

Ride Rating: *Moderate*
Riding Time: *2-3 hours*
Calories Burned: *700*

Terrain

The majority of the ride is along quiet country roads with little car traffic, although there is a short stretch along busy Pacheco Pass Road. It is good any time of year, but best in the springtime when the hillsides are green with new growth.

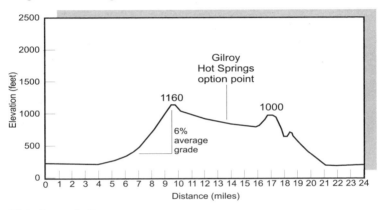

Ride Description

The city of Gilroy was named to honor one of its early residents, John Gilroy. A soap-maker and millwright by trade, Gilroy's main claim to fame seems to have been his marriage to the daughter of Ygnacio Ortega, the owner of Rancho San Ysidro, a 4,460-acre property. Gilroy became part owner of the rancho when Ygnacio died in 1833. However, he ultimately died in poverty at the age of 73 in 1869. His true character may have been revealed by the fact that his real name was Cameron and he only took the name, Gilroy, his mother's maiden name, to avoid capture after jumping ship in Monterey in 1814.

This ride starts in central Gilroy and follows beautiful remote country roads east of town and up into the hills. Cañada Road and Gilroy Hot Springs Road meander through wooded ranch lands with little or no car traffic. There is a substantial hill climb of about 800 feet to get up to these roads, but then they follow a generally flat to rolling route until coming back down into Gilroy.

The route leaves town heading directly east on 6th Street and then Gilman Road. Holsclaw Road leads to Pacheco Pass Road, a busy highway which leads to Cañada Road and out into the rural areas. At Gilroy Hot Springs Road, there is an extra option — out-and-back to the end of the road, where the old Gilroy Hot Springs can be found. Although it is closed to the public, the hot springs provides an interesting goal for those wishing more miles. The route back is along Gilroy Hot Springs Road, Leavesley Road, and Dryden Road.

Starting Point

To get to Gilroy, take Highway 101 south from San Jose and get off at the Leavesley Road exit for Gilroy. Turn right on Leavesley Road toward Monterey Road. Turn left on Monterey Road and then right in the town center on 6th Street. Park anywhere nearby and start the ride at the intersection of 6th Street and Monterey Road.

Ride Details and Mile Markers

0.0   Proceed EAST on 6th Street, heading out of town.

0.5   Cross Highway 101 and begin Gilman Road.

1.6   Turn RIGHT onto Holsclaw Road.

3.1   Turn LEFT onto busy Pacheco Pass Road. Walk your bikes across the intersection for safety.

4.4   Bear RIGHT to stay on Pacheco Pass Road. Ferguson Road is on the left side.

4.8   Turn LEFT onto Cañada Road.

8.9   Top of the climb — 1,200 feet.

10.6   Turn LEFT to stay on Cañada Road as Jamison Road is straight ahead.

13.6   Turn LEFT onto Gilroy Hot Springs Road. Extra option to Gilroy Hot Springs starts here.

16.2   Continue STRAIGHT at the intersection with Coyote Reservoir Road on the right side.

17.6   Continue STRAIGHT to get on Leavesley Road. Roop Road is to the right.

19.3   Turn RIGHT onto Crews Road and continue as Crews Road becomes Dryden Avenue.

20.6   Turn LEFT onto New Avenue.

20.9   Turn RIGHT onto Leavesley Road.

21.2   Turn LEFT onto Holsclaw Road.

22.4   Turn RIGHT onto Gilman Road and re-trace your earlier route into town.

24.0   End of the ride.

Extra Option to Gilroy Hot Springs (3 miles out-and-back)

At the 13.6 mile point, there is an extra option to follow Gilroy Hot Springs Road out to its end at the old Gilroy Hot Springs. Formerly a resort, the hot springs has gone into a state of disrepair and is closed to the public. The option is about 3 miles out to the end and then back along the same road to resume the main ride.

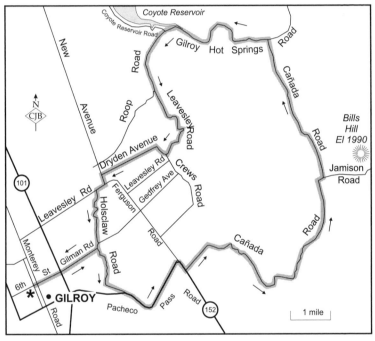

Ride No. 26

27 APTOS
Corralitos and Green Valley Loop

Region: *Watsonville Area*
Total Distance: *35 miles*
Total Elevation Gain: *1400 feet*
Type of Bike: *Road Bike*

Ride Rating: *Moderate*
Riding Time: *4 hours*
Calories Burned: *1000*
Easy Option: *12 miles*

Terrain

There are no serious hill climbs on this ride, but the constantly rolling terrain will be a challenge to most cyclists. The orchards are especially beautiful in the spring when the blossom are fullest, but this ride can be enjoyed any time of year.

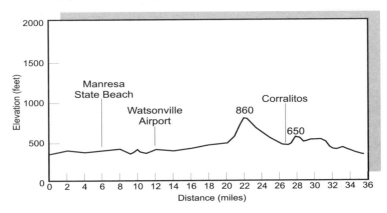

Ride Description

Corralitos is a small farming community located between Santa Cruz and Watsonville. The area around Corralitos is very popular with local cyclists. The roads meander over gently rolling hills through strawberry fields, apple orchards and dense redwood forests at the foot of Mount Madonna.

This ride starts in Aptos, just north and west of Corralitos. It follows Soquel Drive to the residential community of Rio Del Mar, from which it passes the golf course on the way toward Seascape. From there, the route takes you past Manresa State Beach and through the tiny community of La Selva Beach.

Buena Vista Drive will lead you across Highway 1 inland and directly past the Watsonville Airport. After passing through Freedom, the route then follows Green Valley Road back through apple orchards and into the forest. A hill on Hazel Dell Road leads to Brown's Valley

Road for the return toward Corralitos and its landmark grocery store, a good place to take a break and have a snack.

Hames Road, Freedom Boulevard, Day Valley Road, and finally, Valencia Road comprise the route back to Soquel Drive and the return to Aptos.

Starting Point

Start in Aptos at the Rio Rancho Shopping Center on Soquel Drive. To get there, take Highway 1 south from Santa Cruz and get off at the exit for Seacliff Beach and Aptos. Turn left onto State Park Drive and follow it a short distance to Soquel Drive, where the shopping center is on the right. Park in an out-of-the-way spot and begin the ride here.

Ride Details and Mile Markers

0.0 Proceed SOUTH on Soquel Drive.

0.3 Cross under the railroad bridge and bear LEFT to stay on Soquel Drive.

0.5 Continue STRAIGHT at the intersection with Trout Gulch Road.

1.5 Turn RIGHT onto Rio Del Mar Boulevard and cross over Highway 1.

1.7 Turn LEFT onto Club House Drive.

3.3 Turn LEFT onto Sumner Avenue.

Historic site along Valencia Road

3.8   Turn LEFT onto Seascape Boulevard.

4.6   Turn RIGHT onto San Andreas Road.

5.4   Continue STRAIGHT at the intersection with La Playa Boulevard. La Selva Beach is to the right.

6.0   Manresa State Beach on the right side. Public restrooms are available here. **EASY OPTION:** Return from this point.

7.9   Turn LEFT onto Buena Vista Drive.

10.4   Cross under Highway 1.

10.9   Continue STRAIGHT at the intersection with Larkin Valley Road.

11.9   Watsonville Airport is on the right side.

12.7   Turn RIGHT onto Freedom Boulevard and then LEFT onto Airport Boulevard.

13.4   Turn LEFT onto Green Valley Road.

15.5   Bear LEFT to stay on Green Valley Road at the intersection with Casserly Road.

20.5   Turn LEFT onto Hazel Dell Road at the end of Green Valley Road.

23.5   Continue STRAIGHT as the road name changes to Brown's Valley Road.

26.8   Turn RIGHT to stay on Brown's Valley Road and cross over the bridge.

27.0   Corralitos grocery store. Continue STRAIGHT on Hames Road.

28.5   Stay on Hames Road as it turns sharply to the right and then to the left.

29.2   Turn RIGHT onto Freedom Boulevard and then RIGHT again onto Day Valley Road.

31.3   Turn RIGHT onto Valencia Road.

34.0   Turn LEFT onto Trout Gulch Road.

34.5   Turn RIGHT onto Soquel Drive.

34.6   Back at the start point.

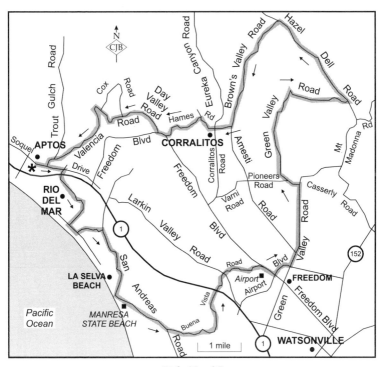

Ride No. 27

28   RIO DEL MAR
Rio Del Mar — Watsonville Loop

Region: *Watsonville Area*
Total Distance: *24 miles*
Total Elevation Gain: *600 feet*
Type of Bike: *Road Bike*

Ride Rating: *Easy*
Riding Time: *2-3 hours*
Calories Burned: *600*

Terrain

There is substantial car traffic in places along this route, but the roads generally are rural and quiet. The terrain is mostly small rolling hills with no difficult climbs.

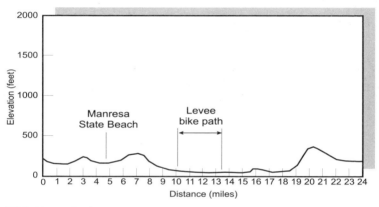

Ride Description

In 1852, Judge John H. Watson and D.S. Gregory laid out the town of Watsonville. The first apple orchard was planted in 1853 and in the following years the town would see its reputation as a productive farming community grow as fast as its fruits and vegetables.

This ride starts in Rio Del Mar and leads south along the coast past Manresa and Sunset State Beaches to Pajaro Dunes, a resort community at the mouth of the Pajaro River. It then follows along a bike path on the levee by the river inland to Watsonville and passes many of the farms and canning factories that support the local economy.

From Watsonville, the route heads north through the rural country-side of Larkin Valley and returns to Rio Del Mar.

Starting Point

The starting point for the ride is at the Deer Park Shopping Mall in Rio Del Mar, just off Highway 1. To get there, take Highway 1 south from Santa Cruz to the Rio Del Mar exit at Rio Del Mar Boulevard. Turn right onto Rio Del Mar Boulevard and then turn right almost immediately into the shopping center. Be sure to park in a spot that does not impact the local shoppers and start the ride here.

Ride Details and Mile Markers

0.0 Turn RIGHT out of the shopping center on Rio Del Mar Boulevard.

0.4 Golf course.

0.5 Turn LEFT onto Sumner Avenue.

1.8 Continue STRAIGHT at the intersection with Club House Drive.

2.3 Turn LEFT at Seascape Boulevard and climb a small hill.

3.1 Turn RIGHT onto San Andreas Road.

3.9 Continue STRAIGHT at the intersection with La Playa Boulevard. La Selva Beach is to the right.

4.6 Manresa State Beach is on the right side.

6.4 Buena Vista Drive is on the left side.

9.8 Turn LEFT at the end of the road onto Beach Road. Pajaro Dunes Beach is at the end of the road to the right.

9.9 Turn RIGHT onto Thurwachter Road and then turn LEFT on the bike path by the river. Farms will then be on your left side and the river will be on your right.

11.2 Highway 1 underpass.

12.9 Turn LEFT onto Walker Street and the gate and railroad tracks.

13.4 Continue STRAIGHT across Beach Road.

13.8 Begin Harkins Slough Road.

14.9 Turn RIGHT onto Green Valley Road.

15.2 Turn LEFT onto Main Street (Highway 152).

15.5 Turn RIGHT onto Holm Road and then turn LEFT immediately onto Westgate Drive.

16.0 Cross Airport Boulevard and begin Larkin Valley Road.

17.2 Continue STRAIGHT across Buena Vista Road.

19.8 Intersection with Mar Monte Drive on the left side.

20.2 Intersection with White Road on the right side.

21.4 Road crosses under Highway 1 and becomes San Andreas Road.

21.6 Turn RIGHT onto Bonita Drive.

22.8 Continue STRAIGHT at the intersection with Freedom Boulevard.

23.7 Cross Club House Drive.

23.8 End of the ride at the shopping center.

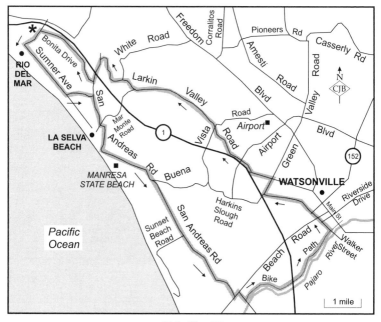

Ride No. 28

29 PAJARO

Pajaro Valley and the Elkhorn Slough

Region: *Watsonville Area*
Total Distance: *25 miles*
Total Elevation Gain: *700 feet*
Type of Bike: *Road Bike*

Ride Rating: *Easy*
Riding Time: *3 hours*
Calories Burned: *600*

Terrain

By virtue of the gently rolling hills with no major climbs, this ride is a very easy one. Most of the roads, with the exception of Castroville Boulevard and San Juan Road, have little car traffic and each of these has a wide shoulder for safety. There are few services along the route, so expect to be self-sufficient.

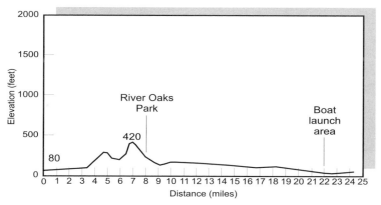

Ride Description

The Elkhorn Slough is one of the few remaining undisturbed wetlands in California and serves as a major link in the Pacific Flyway for migrating birds. If consists of about 2,500 acres of mudflats and coastal tidelands and supports a diverse ecosystem. The name probably comes from the tule elk herds that once roamed the area and served as a part of the diet of the Ohlone Indians some 10,000 to 15,000 years ago.

Occupying the eastern edge of the slough, The Elkhorn Slough National Estuarine Research Reserve was established in 1979. Comprising 1,300 acres, it is used as a research center for this rich and diverse national treasure. There is a visitor center in the reserve that offers interpretive displays demonstrating the workings of the wetlands. Here is also a raised-relief model of the spectacular undersea Monterey Canyon.

The ride starts out at the Elkhorn Slough Reserve Visitor Center and leads south along Elkhorn Road to Castroville Boulevard. The route then heads east for a short distance and then north along a series of rural and residential roads towards the small town of Pajaro (Spanish for "bird"). Salinas Road then takes you south to Elkhorn Road and the return to the visitor center.

Starting Point

Start the ride at the Elkhorn Slough Reserve Visitor Center. To get there, head south on Highway 1 from Santa Cruz. Turn left onto Dolan Road just after you cross the bridge over the Elkhorn Slough. After about 3 miles, turn left onto Elkhorn Road. Another 2 miles gets you to the visitor center on the left side. This is a good place to explore either before or after your ride.

An alternate way to get there is to follow Highway 101 south from San Jose, exiting at Castroville Boulevard and proceeding west. From this direction, you turn right onto Elkhorn Road after about 4 miles.

Ride Details and Mile Markers

0.0   Proceed SOUTH along Elkhorn Road.

2.0   Turn LEFT onto Castroville Boulevard.

3.4   Paradise Road intersection on the left side.

5.1   Turn LEFT onto San Miguel Canyon Road.

6.0   Turn RIGHT onto Echo Valley Road.

6.5   Turn LEFT onto Maher Road and climb a short hill.

7.6   Royal Oaks Park on the right side. This is a good place to stop for a rest.

9.5   Turn LEFT onto Tarpey Road and then RIGHT onto San Miguel Canyon Road.

10.7 Lewis Road intersection is on the left side.

12.1 Turn LEFT onto Vega Road.

14.4 Turn RIGHT onto Lewis Road.

16.7 Turn LEFT onto Salinas Road.

17.1 Lewis Road intersection is on the left side.

17.9 Turn LEFT onto Elkhorn Road.

18.7 Intersection with Hudson Landing Road on the right side. Cross over the bridge.

18.9 Bear RIGHT to stay on Elkhorn Road at the intersection with Hall Road on the left.

20.9 Elkhorn Slough visible on the right side.

21.7 Boat launch area on the right side.

24.2 Back at the visitor center.

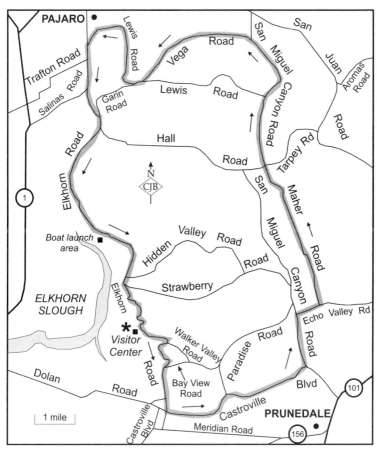

Ride No. 29

30   MORGAN HILL
Henry Coe State Park Out-and-Back

Region: *South County*
Total Distance: *24 miles*
Total Elevation Gain: *2700 feet*
Type of Bike: *Road Bike*

Ride Rating: *Difficult*
Riding Time: *4 hours*
Calories Burned: *1200*

Terrain

The route of this ride is an out-and-back along East Dunne Avenue east of Morgan Hill. The road is easy to follow and carries little car traffic as it leads first through residential areas and then climbs steadily all the way to the park headquarters for Henry Coe State Park.

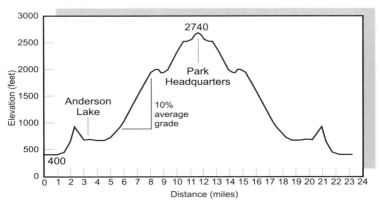

Ride Description

The largest state park in California, encompassing more than 80,000 acres, Henry Coe State Park is rugged and remote, while still being within easy access of the population centers of the Bay Area. Originally home to Ohlone Indians and later a major ranch run by Henry W. Coe, Jr., the land is now populated by wild turkeys, golden eagles, wild pigs and mountain lions, along with a great variety of plants and vegetation. In 1953, Sada Coe, a descendent of Henry, donated the land to the state of California and in 1958 it became a state park. Since then, the park has grown as adjacent properties have been acquired and incorporated into the park.

This ride follows East Dunne Avenue from a point just off Highway 101 in Morgan Hill to the park headquarters at the end of the road, about 12 miles distant. The route first leads through residential neighborhood along a flat stretch of the road and then climbs to another residential area in the hills overlooking Anderson Lake. After descending to a bridge across Coyote Creek at the inlet to the lake, the road then becomes much more remote as it climbs through ranch land and past hillsides studded with oaks and madrone.

The climbing is aggressive and relentless and the workout is rewarded at the end by a visit at the well-maintained visitor center at the park. Here there are some of the original ranch buildings which you can explore and a small museum and gift shop. A visit here can serve as a pleasant break in your workout before you begin the long descent back to the start point.

Starting Point

The ride begins in Morgan Hill, just off Highway 101 south of San Jose. To get there, take Highway 101 south and get off at the exit for East Dunne Avenue. Proceed east on East Dunne Avenue and cross over the freeway. Begin the ride at the corner of East Dunne Avenue and Murphy Avenue.

Ride Details and Mile Markers

0.0 Proceed EAST along East Dunne Avenue, away from the freeway.

1.2 Begin the first climb. It is short but steep.

2.5 At the top of the hill, bear slightly RIGHT to stay on East Dunne Avenue and begin to descend.

3.7 Cross over the Cochrane Bridge.

5.4 Sharp hairpin turn to the right and then begin to climb more steeply.

6.4 Sharp hairpin turn to the left.

8.4 Begin a short descent into a small valley and then resume climbing.

10.9 Begin the final steep section to the park.

11.6 End of the road at the park headquarters. Restrooms and water are available and there is a small visitor center that is worth checking out. At the end of your stay here, reverse your route back to Morgan Hill.

23.2 Back at the start point.

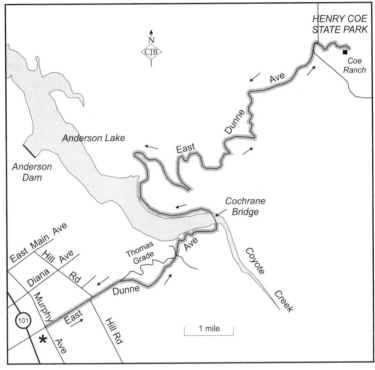

Ride No. 30

31   GILROY

Henry Coe State Park — Kelly Lake

Region: *South County*
Total Distance: *16 miles*
Total Elevation Gain: *2300 feet*
Type of Bike: *Mountain Bike*

Ride Rating: *Difficult*
Riding Time: *3-4 hours*
Calories Burned: *1500*
Easy Option: *7 miles*

Terrain

    This out-and-back ride follows along wide fire roads which are normally very smooth. The trails are well-marked and easy to follow. While there is substantial climbing, the grades are not terribly steep and no special riding skills are needed. Summer days can be quite hot and dry, so be prepared with adequate water and food. Springtime is the best time for this ride, when the streams are full and the hillsides are green.

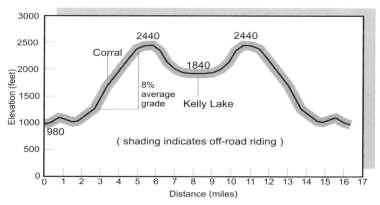

Ride Description

    Henry Coe State Park lies about 4 miles east of Morgan Hill and Gilroy, in the southernmost part of Santa Clara County. Formerly an operating ranch owned by Henry W. Coe, the park today is one of the largest state parks in northern California and continues to grow as new lands are acquired on a fairly regular basis.

    The southern section of the park, not nearly as well-known as the northern section, is the focus of this ride. There is an entrance into the park near the once famous Gilroy Hot Springs at the end of Gilroy Hot Springs Road. No services are available at this end of the park, so be sure to bring adequate water and snacks.

    The ride follows a simple out-and-back route to pristine Kelly Lake along wide fire roads. The start of the ride is flat as it follows along

Coyote Creek. Early in the ride, the old buildings of Gilroy Hot Springs can be seen across the creek and in the distance. About 3 miles into the ride, the fire road climbs as it heads away from the creek and up toward the ridge. Near the top, the trail then follows along the ridge line and offers spectacular views in both directions. The descent is an easy one and is followed by a short stretch along another creek leading to Kelly Lake.

Starting Point

Take Highway 101 south to Gilroy. Get off at Leavesley Road and follow it east about 2 miles. Turn left onto New Avenue and then right onto Roop Road. Follow Roop Road and then Gilroy Hot Springs Road, all the way to the end. Park along the road and look for the gate on the right side, leading into the park.

Ride Details and Mile Markers

0.0   Proceed EAST into the park on the fire road on the right side of the road.

0.1   Bear LEFT at the trail split and enter the park.

0.7   Views of the old Gilroy Hot Springs buildings off to the left.

2.2   Begin climbing.

3.3   Coit Camp and corral on the left side. **EASY OPTION:** Return from this point.

4.0   Turn RIGHT at the major trail intersection, heading toward Kelly Lake.

4.3   Cross Canyon Trail West intersection on the left side.

5.0   Single-track trail intersection on the right side.

5.9   Continue STRAIGHT at Jackson Trail junction on the right side.

7.2   Follow the trail along the stream after the long descent.

7.6   Cross the stream.

7.8   Turn RIGHT to get to Kelly Lake.

8.0   Kelly Lake. When you complete your stay at the lake, turn around and return the way you came.

16.0   Back at the start point.

Building at the historic Coe Ranch ⇨

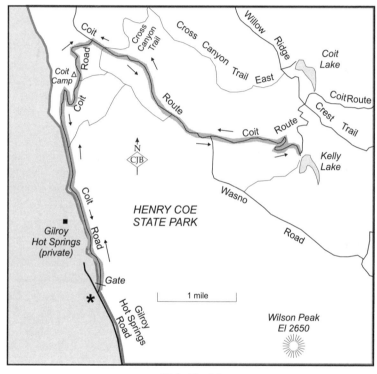

Ride No. 31

APPENDIX

RIDES BY RATINGS

Easiest Rides (short options on longer rides)
(short rides, flat or with some small grades)

1. San Felipe Valley and Metcalf Road (12 miles). 11
3. Coyote Creek Bike Path (13 miles) 18
5. Sierra Road Loop (6 miles). 24
6. Grant Ranch County Park (7 miles) 27
9. Los Gatos Creek Trail (9 miles) 39
12. St. Joseph's Hill Open Space Preserve (4 miles) 49
13. Los Gatos and Soquel Loop (9 miles) 54
14. Santa Cruz and Capitola Beach Ride (12 miles) 57
16. Seacliff Beach and Corralitos Loop (7 miles) 63
18. The Forest of Nisene Marks and Sand Point Overlook
     (9 miles). 69
21. Felton Empire Road (13 miles). 80
24. Wilder Ranch (3 miles). 90
27. Corralitos and Green Valley Loop (12 miles) 102
31. Henry Coe State Park — Kelly Lake (7 miles) 115

Easy Rides
(medium rides, mostly flat or with some moderate grades)

3. Coyote Creek Bike Path (31 miles) 18
9. Los Gatos Creek Trail (17 miles). 39
14. Santa Cruz and Capitola Beach Ride (23 miles) 57
25. Chesbro and Uvas Reservoirs (19 miles) 95
28. Rio Del Mar — Watsonville Loop (24 miles) 106
29. Pajaro Valley and the Elkhorn Slough (25 miles) 109

Moderate Rides
(15-20 mile rides with small to moderate hill climbs)

1. San Felipe Valley and Metcalf Road (22 miles). 11
2. New Almaden and Hicks Road Loop (19 miles) 14
7. Saratoga and Stevens Canyon Back Roads (15 miles). 32
8. Tour of Los Gatos and Saratoga Foothills (23 miles). 35
12. St. Joseph's Hill Open Space Preserve (6 miles) 49
16. Seacliff Beach and Corralitos Loop (21 miles) 63
18. The Forest of Nisene Marks and Sand Point Overlook
     (17 miles). 69
23. Big Basin Redwoods State Park (16 miles) 86
24. Wilder Ranch (18 miles). 90
26. Gilroy Hot Springs and Cañada Road (23 miles). 98
27. Corralitos and Green Valley Loop (35 miles) 102

Difficult Rides
(long distances, with challenging sustained climbs)

4. Quimby Road Loop (21 miles) 21
5. Sierra Road Loop (16 miles) 24
6. Grant Ranch County Park(16 miles) 27
10. Los Gatos and Castle Rock Loop (36 miles) 43
11. Sierra Azul Open Space Preserve (16 miles) 46
13. Los Gatos and Soquel Loop (50 miles) 54
15. Eureka Canyon and Soquel Loop (40 miles) 60
17. Soquel Demonstration Forest (13 miles) 66
19. Empire Grade and Bonny Doon (27 miles) 74
20. Zayante Road and Bear Creek Road Loop (28 miles) 77
21. Felton Empire Road (30 miles). 80
22. Big Basin and Castle Rock Loop (43 miles) 83
30. Henry Coe State Park Out-and-Back (24 miles). 112
31. Henry Coe State Park — Kelly Lake (16 miles) 115

MOUNTAIN BIKE TRAILS
(off-road rides on trails or fire roads)

6. Grant Ranch County Park (Easiest, Difficult) 27
11. Sierra Azul Open Space Preserve (Difficult) 46
12. St. Joseph's Hill Open Space Preserve (Easiest, Moderate). . . 49
17. Soquel Demonstration Forest (Difficult) 66
18. The Forest of Nisene Marks and Sand Point Overlook
    (Easiest, Moderate) 69
23. Big Basin Redwoods State Park (Moderate) 86
24. Wilder Ranch (Easiest, Moderate) 90
31. Henry Coe State Park — Kelly Lake (Easiest, Difficult). . . . 115

POINTS OF INTEREST

State Parks

Big Basin Redwoods State Park
  Highway 235, Big Basin
  (831) 338-8860
  Hiking, camping, mountain
  biking

Henry W. Coe State Park
  End of East Dunne Avenue,
  Morgan Hill
  (408) 779-2728
  Hiking, camping, mountain
  biking

Henry Cowell Redwoods State Park
  Highway 9, Felton
  (831) 335-4598
  Hiking, camping, mountain
  biking

*The Forest of Nisene Marks State
Park*
  Soquel Drive, Aptos
  (831) 763-7062
  Hiking, camping, mountain
  biking

Natural Bridges State Beach
  Swanton Blvd., Santa Cruz
  (831) 423-4609
  Winter home of Monarch
  butterflies

Seacliff State Beach
  State Park Drive, Aptos
  (831) 429-2850
  Home of the cement ship,
  Palo Alto

Soquel Demonstration Forest
  Highland Way, Soquel
  (831) 475-8643
  Hiking, mountain biking

Wilder Ranch State Park
  Highway 1, north of Santa Cruz
  (831) 423-9703
  Cultural preserve with hiking,
  mountain biking

Santa Clara County Parks
  Santa Clara County Parks
  Commission
  (408) 299-2323

Almaden Quicksilver County Park
  Almaden Road, San Jose
  (408) 268-8338
  Hiking, equestrian

Ed R. Levin County Park
  Calaveras Road, Milpitas
  (408) 262-6980
  Hiking, equestrian, picnicking

Joseph D. Grant County Park
  Mount Hamilton Road, San Jose
  (408) 358-3741
  Hiking, equestrian, mountain
  biking

Mount Madonna County Park
  Pole Line Road, Morgan Hill
  (408) 842-2341
  Hiking, equestrian, mountain
  biking, picnicking

Stevens Canyon County Park
  Stevens Canyon Road,
  Cupertino
  (408) 358-3751
  Hiking, equestrian, picnicking

Uvas Canyon County Park
  Croy Road, Morgan Hill
  (408) 779-9232
  Hiking, picnicking

Villa Montalvo Arboretum
  Montalvo Road, Saratoga
  (408) 867-0190
  Art gallery, hiking trails,
  arboretum

Selected Wineries

Bargetto Winery
  3535 North Main Street, Soquel
  (831) 475-2258

Bonny Doon Vineyard
10 Pine Flat Road, Santa Cruz
(831) 425-3625

Byington Winery
21850 Bear Creek Road,
Los Gatos
(408) 354-1111

Hallcrest Vineyards
379 Felton Empire Road, Felton
(831) 335-4441

Hecker Pass Winery
4605 Hecker Pass Road, Gilroy
(408) 842-8755

Kirigin Cellars
11550 Watsonville Road, Gilroy
(408) 847-8827

Ridge Vineyards
17100 Montebello Road,
Cupertino
(408) 867-3723

Sycamore Creek Vineyards
12775 Uvas Road, Morgan Hill
(408) 779-4783

Miscellaneous

Elkhorn Slough National Estuarine
Research Reserve
1700 Elkhorn Road,
Watsonville
(831) 728-2822
Bird watching and learning
center

Opry House at Club Almaden
21350 Almaden Road, San Jose
(408) 268-2492
Historic restaurant and
melodrama theater

Roaring Camp & Big Trees Narrow
Gauge Railroad
Graham Hill Road, Felton
(831) 335-4400
Steam train rides

Midpeninsula Regional Open Space
District
Palo Alto
(650) 949-5500
Administration of open space
properties

The Elkhorn Slough

BICYCLING TIPS

Familiarize yourself with these simple tips to make yourself a better and safer cyclist.

GENERAL RULES OF THE ROAD

1. Always ride on the right side of the road and never against the flow of traffic. Remember that bicycles are subject to the same laws as cars.

2. Keep as far to the right as possible in order to allow cars sufficient room to pass. Always ride in single file when traffic is present.

3. Signal when you are turning or slowing down in order to allow following riders to prepare for the same and to indicate to cars what you are doing. Never act suddenly, except in an emergency.

4. Never ride on freeways except where bicycles are specifically permitted.

5. Cross railroad tracks and cattle guards perpendicularly. In wet conditions, these may be very slippery and it may be necessary to walk your bike across to ensure your safety.

6. In rain or in wet road conditions, ride slower and more cautiously then you normally would. Not only are the pavements slippery, but your brakes will not grab as well when they are wet.

7. Avoid night riding. If you absolutely must, be sure to wear bright clothing and to carry a flashing light.

8. Never assume that another car or cyclist will yield to you. Ride assertively, but be cautious and defensive.

9. Use extra care when passing parked cars. Watch for doors to open suddenly.

10. Avoid riding on sidewalks unless signs indicate that bicycles are permitted or if traffic conditions are so dangerous that you have no choice.

11. When making a left turn in traffic, ride assertively and give clear signals as to your intentions. Be courteous and show appreciation when a vehicle pauses to give you clearance.

12. Always stop at red lights and stop signs. Bicycles have no special privileges.

13. Signal the presence of road debris or potholes to cyclists following behind you.

OFF-ROAD BIKING

1. Know the rules for the area in which you are riding. Always stay on trails intended for bikes. Leave the area just as you found it.

2. Yield to equestrians. Horses may spook when a bicycle appears suddenly. When approaching from behind, talk loudly so the horse can hear you coming. Most horses are familiar with human voices, but not with bicycles.

3. Yield to hikers. It is important to share the trails harmoniously.

4. Always be courteous. Nothing is worse for the sport than hostility among trail users.

5. Look ahead to anticipate encounters. Approach blind curves slowly.

6. Avoid contact with plant life along the trails. Poison oak is very common in northern California and can be a very unpleasant experience.

7. Carry maps at all times, unless you are very familiar with the area.

8. Mountain bike tires can be deflated a small amount to provide for better traction in loose conditions.

9. Lower your saddle before you begin a steep downhill. This will give you a lower center of gravity and will reduce the chance of your being launched over the handlebars if you hit an obstacle.

EQUIPMENT

1. Always carry a spare tube, patch kit, pump and tools.

2. Be prepared to fix your own bike if problems arise. Don't depend on others to do this for you unless you have a tacit understanding.

3. Check your equipment before you go, not after you are underway. Check for tire pressure and for proper operation of brakes and gear shifters.

4. Road riding requires fully inflated tires. Soft tires can result in punctures when sharp bumps or potholes are encountered.

5. Carry adequate amounts of water.

6. If you ride at night, make sure your bike is equipped with reflectors.

7. Toe clips or clipless pedals are much more comfortable than flat pedals, especially on long rides. They make climbing easier, too.

8. A rear view mirror is a useful accessory by permitting you to see approaching cyclists and vehicles without turning around.

9. Carry a lock when you expect to leave your bike unattended.

CLOTHING

1. A helmet is mandatory for obvious safety reasons.
2. Wear bright clothing that can be easily seen by motorists.
3. Lycra shorts offer more comfort on long rides than loose fitting shorts.
4. Gloves are not absolutely necessary, but can help you avoid blisters or blood circulation problems.
5. Carry a lightweight windbreaker if you expect to encounter changing weather conditions.
6. Wear goggles or some other form of eyewear to protect your eyes from the harmful effects of the sun and from dirt and debris that may be present.

TECHNIQUE

1. A properly adjusted seat height will ensure your comfort and will help to avoid knee injuries. The correct height will result in a slight bend in the knee when the leg is fully extended to the lower of the two pedals.
2. Be familiar with gear shifting so you can anticipate the hill climbs and shift before you need to. It is sometimes difficult to shift when you are in the middle of a steep climb. Always keep the pedals moving when you shift.
3. The upright position on dropped handlebars is usually the most comfortable position for most road riding. Position yourself on the lower part of the bars when you are going downhill to get the most leverage on the brakes.
4. When riding in a group, it is both safe and polite to regroup frequently. Avoid getting spread out over long distances.

ABOUT THE AUTHOR

Born in New Jersey in 1943, Conrad Boisvert has been a resident of the Bay Area since 1972. With a long career as an electronics engineer, he has been a recreational cyclist for many years. Not only has he toured the many roads and trails in and around the Bay Area, but he has also cycled extensively in other states and internationally, as well. He currently resides in Aptos.

The author in Death Valley

THE BAY AREA BIKE TRAILS SERIES

The Bay Area Bike Trails Series offers over 175 self-guided road and mountain bicycle tours. Each ride contains clear, detailed maps, easily followed directions with mile markers, elevation profiles of the terrain, beautiful photographs, historical background and points of interest.

Bay Area Mountain Bike Trails by Conrad J. Boisvert, 1993 (latest revision 2000). $16.95. The Bay Area offers some of the most exciting and scenic off-road trails and a wealth of hidden trails, all within easy access of major cities. From Santa Rosa south to Gilroy, you can ride along the spectacular ridges of Mt. Tamalpais, view the Golden Gate Bridge from the Marin Headlands, or challenge yourself on the hills of Mt. Diablo.

East Bay Bike Trails by Conrad J. Boisvert, 1992 (latest revision 1993). $12.95. Somewhat sheltered from coastal fog and ocean winds, the East Bay extends from the Carquinez Strait south to Fremont. Interesting bike routes take you through heavily wooded hills above Oakland and Berkeley, orchards and farms around Brentwood, eerie windmills in Livermore, the wetlands around Newark, and dramatic Mount Diablo in Danville.

Marin County Bike Trails by Phyllis L. Neumann, 1989 (latest revision 1996). $12.95. Just across the Golden Gate Bridge, Marin County combines exquisite natural beauty with sophisticated elegance to give you spectacular views, rugged cliffs, natural beaches, well-developed parks, rural farmlands, tiny hidden towns and Mt. Tamalpais. A specially designed bike route from Petaluma to the Golden Gate Bridge is also included.

San Francisco Peninsula Bike Trails by Conrad J. Boisvert, 1991 (latest revision 1993). $11.95. Few areas can compare with the spectacular San Francisco Peninsula, which encompasses the wooded foothills around Woodside, dense redwood forests in the Santa Cruz mountains and remote country roads along the rugged Pacific coastline.

Sonoma County Bike Trails, 3rd Edition by Phyllis L. Neumann, 1999. $13.95. Less than an hour's drive north from San Francisco brings you to tranquil country roads, gently rolling farmlands, towering redwoods, lush vineyards, local wineries, the Russian River and the Pacific coastline. A specially designed bike route from Cloverdale to Petaluma is also included.

South Bay Bike Trails, 2nd Edition by Conrad J. Boisvert, 2000. $14.95. Better known for its high-tech image, once you head out into the surrounding countryside, the South Bay is a cyclist's paradise. From San Jose south to Gilroy, picturesque rides take you through ranchlands around Morgan Hill, dense redwood forests in the Santa Cruz mountains, and the coastal wetlands of the Elkhorn Slough. Heading south along the Pacific coast brings you to the famous seaside resorts and beaches of Santa Cruz and Capitola.